CREATIVE PASTORAL CARE AND COUNSELING SERIES

PASTORAL CARE AND COUNSELING WITH LATINO/AS

R. Esteban Montilla and Ferney Medina

FORTRESS PRESS   MINNEAPOLIS

PASTORAL CARE AND COUNSELING WITH LATINO/AS
Creative Pastoral Care and Counseling Series

See page 146 for a list of biblical references.

R. Esteban Montilla has also published a book that relates to topics of chapter 1. Montilla, R., and R. Smith, ed. (2005). *Counseling and Family Therapy with Latino Populations: Strategies That Work*. New York: Routledge.

Cover photo: © Stockbyte Gold / Getty Images. Used by permission.
Author photos: Ferney Medina, © Felix Studio; R. Esteban Montilla, © Kristi Morales. Used by permission.

Library of Congress Cataloging-in-Publication Data

Montilla, R. Esteban.
   Pastoral care and counseling with Latino/as / R. Esteban Montilla and Ferney Medina.
      p. cm. — (Creative pastoral care and counseling series)
   Includes bibliographical references.
   ISBN 0-8006-3820-4 (alk. paper)
   1. Church work with Hispanic Americans. 2. Pastoral care. 3. Pastoral counseling. I. Medina, Ferney. II. Title. III. Series.

   BV4468.2.H57M65 2006
   259.089'68073—dc22
                              2006003751

Manufactured in the U.S.A.

CONTENTS

/520

124 069

EDITOR'S FOREWORD

The growing Latino/a influence on American culture is impossible to ignore—certainly for those of us living in Texas and the other border states. All we have to do is glance around us. But this trend goes far beyond the border states. What was once a south-of-the-border culture has now spread throughout all of North America. Residents of Latin American descent now make up more than 13 percent of the population of the United States.

Esteban Montilla and Ferney Medina set out to help readers of all backgrounds to develop "cultural empathy" for the many aspects of Latin culture. This is not a single tradition with specific practices and mores, but actually a great number of overlapping cultures possessing many similarities, to be sure, but also significant differences. The authors point out that the "Latino population is a polyculture combining a very heterogeneous and multicolor group of people with a combination of ethnicities, an array of languages, a variety of religions, and of diverse socioeconomic and educational status that, although diverse, maintain distinctive features and principles that make it 'one' particular people."

The influence of Latin culture also affects the church and its ministry. *Pastoral Care and Counseling with Latino/as* addresses these changes. It suggests ways in which we can reshape the pastoral care ministry that most of us learned in seminary and graduate school to address anew those we serve who have Latin American heritage. In doing so, we can enrich our own lives and ministries in countless ways.

Montilla is not a shy or retiring person. He called me, out of the blue, because he had read my books and wanted me to make a presentation to some Spanish-speaking ministers and chaplains in the border lands between Texas and Mexico. I agreed to do it.

Quickly abandoning my dismal Spanish, I addressed the group in English and relied on Montilla to translate on the spot. I began to notice that some of his translations took considerably longer than my English version. As the day wore on it dawned on me that he was expressing my ideas better, and in greater detail, than I had. He seemed to know the material in my books as well or better than I!

Over the years since that first meeting, I have come to know Montilla as a friend as well as a respected colleague. He is one of the brightest thinkers I know in the field of pastoral care. He is very well read—in both the English- and Spanish-language literature—and can speak cross-culturally and articulately to issues facing pastoral care in our rapidly changing, real-world ministry.

Montilla is not only a thinker but also a doer, and he writes about what he is doing. He has served as a hospital chaplain for twelve years. Several years ago he established a pastoral care and counseling education program in Spanish on the border of Texas and Mexico; people of both countries attend. That program will soon grow into a complete Master of Divinity degree program. He has done the same in Venezuela; I had the good fortune to attend the graduation of the first M.Div. class in December 2004. Yet another M.Div. program is under development in El Salvador; the first students will enter that program soon after this book is released. All along, Montilla has also been doing some of this work in conjunction with Brite Divinity School, Texas Christian University, and the Ecumenical Center for Religion and Health.

That's a lot of irons in the fire. Like many effective people with wide-ranging interests and commitments, Montilla surrounds himself with good people to help make his vision a successful reality. One of those individuals is Ferney Medina. Medina is another gifted pastoral caregiver from Medellín, Colombia, who started studying with Montilla four years ago and is completing his training as clinical pastoral supervisor. As a pastoral counselor and chaplain serving Latinos and Latinas on the border, Medina is recognized and respected for his leadership in ministry and education, reflecting the essence of what it means to be a pastor.

In *Pastoral Care and Counseling with Latino/as*, Montilla and Medina have given us a comprehensive guide for pastoral care ministry with individuals and families of Latin American descent. It offers ways to approach the Hispanic family with respect, honoring individual traditions and values and remaining aware of the role of faith and family in the suffering and healing of people. The authors do a great deal to help sensitize the reader to this diversity.

I am confident that reading *Pastoral Care and Counseling with Latino/as* will strengthen and enrich your pastoral care, counseling, and general ministry. Montilla and Medina bring to their work the wisdom of many years of experience as pastors, chaplains, and teachers. The scope and quality of the care you offer to an increasingly diverse population is certain to benefit from their knowledge and sound guidance.

HOWARD W. STONE

PREFACE

The growth, expansion, and strengthening of the Latino/a community is a reality that is overtaking the United States at a dramatic pace. We need not refer to statistical data to convey the rapid growth of our Latino/a people. We probably just need to look around to see face-to-face the changing appearance of what used to be an overwhelmingly homogeneous society. This rapid change is certainly threatening to those who do not dare to explore the possibilities that accompany such an influx of peoples, colors, languages, and ideologies. But the polycultural experience that shapes the countenance of the Latino/a community constitutes a limitless resource available to those brave enough to venture into the challenge of befriending this diverse group of peoples.

This challenge is even more significant if we consider the nontraditional characteristics of the emerging Latino/a community in our time. Nowadays, we encounter educated, English-speaking, organized, and successful Latino/as in almost every field of our American society. The stereotypical depiction of the lazy, uneducated, and passive Latino/a is proving to be a myth that needs to be reevaluated. The Latino/a community is a dormant giant that little by little is awakening to the power and influence that, because of its condition, it is investing in every single institution of our American way of living.

Pastoral care is one of the institutions being profoundly affected by this change. This is especially true if we consider that, because of their investiture, ministers are predominantly at the forefront of the social and political transformation of our society. Thus, it is a fallacy to think we can continue ministering to Latino/as using the same methods that proved somehow successful in years past. The minister who is, at this day and time, still trading mirrors for gold is simply burying the possibility of serving the real needs of this growing community. By the same token, humbly admitting that there is much we can learn and incorporate into our ministry from this diverse group of peoples represents a cornerstone on which to build the cultural richness of diversity and reciprocity.

This humble approach becomes a priority when we recognize that, in spite of the assimilating efforts of the dominant culture, the Latino/a community maintains the traditions, rituals, languages, foods, and colors that are at its core. More than any other cultural group in America, Latino/as have been able to incorporate their own idiosyncrasies into mainstream American culture. The lineup of television channels in Spanish is considerable. Bilingual advertising is almost a given for many products that are targeting the Latino/a market. Cinco de Mayo has become almost as important a feast as the Fourth of July or Saint Patrick's Day. Mexican food is an undeniable part of our life in America. Latino/a entertainers (musicians, comedians, and actors/actresses) are at the peak of popularity. And the list continues growing and showing the strength of a community that values and remains faithful to most of its traditions while incorporating those that allow its development in this society.

Thus, it is the purpose of this book to enrich systematically the knowledge that you might have accumulated in your ministerial experience, while providing therapeutic tools that are culturally appropriate for Latino/as. By reading this book, you will grow familiar with the most intimate and intricate dynamics of our Latino/a culture. You will learn about *familismo* and the values of *respeto* and loyalty highly regarded in our culture. You will become familiar with the concept of community and its relevance in the healing process of Latino/a individuals. You will be confronted by our autochthonous understanding of illness and suffering. You will also be introduced to the ethos and mores that have been revisited under the idea of solidarity, giving it a new and fresh feeling. You will be challenged by the reality of education and the need to propose a new paradigm of education and learning that reach those who have traditionally been marginalized. Finally, we will discuss the current issue of "cultural discrimination" and the dangers of and alternatives to the concept of assimilation.

We review these topics under a scriptural base that is nonetheless inclusive and welcoming of diversity. This book is not intended as a finished product, since we realize that there is much more to the pastoral care and counseling of Latino/as than what we could pack into these pages. This work, then, serves as an invitation for your own reflection, research, prayer, and pastoral practice. We hope that your ministerial experience or desire to serve and appropriate the richness of the Latino community becomes the motivating factor that makes of these pages a living text full of heart and passion. It is our pleasure and honor to present you with this work born out of the beauty and richness of our Latino people.

Introduction

PASTORAL CARE AND COUNSELING FROM A LATINO/A PERSPECTIVE

Pastoral counseling is about freeing, liberating, and unwrapping people from their cognitive, emotional, relational, and behavioral bondages. This untying process is illustrated in the biblical story about an encounter between Jesus of Nazareth and Lazarus. The gospel relates that Lazarus was dead and was brought back to life by Jesus, who then asked his disciples to unbind Lazarus because he was alive but bound hand and foot with wrappings (John 11:43-45). This is still the responsibility of those who decide to be coworkers with God in the process of setting people free.

During Jesus' time, most people were buried in tomblike structures dug out of the earthen hillsides or, in some places, the soft sandstone, somewhat resembling a cave, in front of which a large stone was rolled to protect the bodies from scavengers and other animals and to show dignity and respect for the dead person. We often visualize the dead being "laid" to rest, with their body in a prone position. In fact, some were laid horizontally, but because of limited space and the custom of that time, some were actually placed vertically, standing in the tomb. The gospel story suggests that Lazarus was standing.

When prepared for burial, the dead were anointed with oils and herbal mixtures by their loved ones or professional embalmers. After preparation, their bodies were wrapped with a gauzy cloth in three sections: the head, the upper body and arms, and the lower trunk and legs. This cloth consisted of long, narrow strips, probably several inches wide and several feet long, which were wrapped tightly around the body of the dead.

The gospel writer tells us that when the stone was removed from the place where Lazarus was laid, Jesus stated in a loud voice, "Lazarus, come out!" The dead man came out, his hands and feet wrapped with strips of linen, and a cloth around his face. Jesus said to them, "Take off the grave clothes and let him go" (John 11:43-45, NIV).

Lazarus was literally raised from the dead! This is something not possible for ordinary humans. He had been dead for four days. The author portrays Jesus as doing that which is impossible for humans but possible for God. Then Jesus asked his disciples to do that which is possible for humans: to untie Lazarus and let him go. We believe that the role of the pastoral counselor is not to "resurrect" people but to unwrap them from their cognitive, emotional, spiritual, and relational bondages. God does the impossible; we don't.

Lazarus was tightly wrapped from the top of his head to the end of his fingers and toes. The only way he could have come out of the tomb under his own steam would have been to sort of hop out, but he did "come forth"! Just imagine Lazarus standing there with Jesus, his sisters, and friends in attendance.

Wrapped as Lazarus was, he could not move his hands, his arms, his legs, or feet. He could not see, due to the wrappings around his head. He could not hear much, due to the cloth wrapped around his head, and he surely could not yet speak, since during the preparation, extra cloth and herbs were normally placed in orifices such as the mouth, eyes, and ears. Lazarus was alive but unable to function.

After Jesus Christ brought Lazarus back to life, he presented Lazarus to his disciples, so they could do what was possible for them to do. When Jesus said to those standing there, "Loose him, and let him go," he was directing that Lazarus be returned to a functional state. Today Jesus trusts us with the same work and commission (Carlson 1994).

Remember, Lazarus had been dead for four days. He had been in a dark tomb with no sunlight reaching his eyes, no sounds reaching his ears. He was in a fragile and vulnerable state. Imagine having had your eyes covered for four days and suddenly being thrust into the bright sunlight, or to have been in complete silence for four days and suddenly being inundated with loud noises. This is what we must remember in the process of unwrapping those to whom we offer our ministry. We must first do no harm.

If we were to unwrap Lazarus quickly—for instance, using a knife to cut through the layers of grave cloths—we might cut him and cause him harm. It is crucial that we go slowly, strip by strip in the unwrapping, and to begin from the top of his head, working gently down to his feet, and to do so with respect.

What would you expect to see when Lazarus was finally unwrapped? He would, of course, be naked. What is it like to be naked in front of others? How would you feel if you found yourself naked in front of others, even if they were your family and loved ones—just standing there naked? Lazarus needs to be dressed again, in order to be reunited with his community.

This gospel story could serve as a metaphor of what pastoral counseling is all about. We all have things that are oppressing us: irrational and illogical beliefs and expectations that affect our lives. We have unresolved hurt and wounds that are a part of us and that may not be bleeding but are still sensitive. These wounds affect our mind, our heart, and our lifestyle, as well as our ministry. They affect how we walk in this world, how we live our life. Sometimes we experience life in such a way that we see the need to walk a different way. But our legs are so accustomed to walking a certain way, they just want to continue to go that way. We need to be unwrapped, to see a new way of walking. We need to be unwrapped from head to toe and to become naked, so to speak. Don't we want to be unwrapped gently and respectfully? We need to be allowed to experience a new way of walking and seeing in order to become reunited with our community, to become whole, and thereby to experience the glory of the reign of God here on earth. And we need this so we can share this experience with others, especially the marginalized of society, those on the periphery. Pastoral counselors are committed to continue this ministry of untying and unwrapping God's people.

BORN TO BE FREE AND WHOLE

Jesus of Nazareth described his liberating and life-giving message using the words of the prophet Isaiah, "The Spirit of the Lord is on me, because he has anointed me to preach good news to the poor. He has sent me to *proclaim freedom for the prisoners* and recovery of sight for the blind, *to release the oppressed*, to proclaim the year of the Lord's favor" (Luke 4:18-19, NIV, italics added).

Latino theologian Leonardo Boff (2002) illustrates the liberating message of the gospel through a metaphor initially told by James Aggrey (1875–1927) to help his people understand what it means to be free. Aggrey was born in Ghana, a small country in Africa, and was a teacher and missionary who attended Livingstone College and received his doctorate degree from Columbia University. His dream was to see a free and sovereign Ghana. Sadly,

Aggrey died in 1927 before his dream was realized, but he had planted the seed. The liberation came years later in 1957, when Ghana proclaimed its independence and regained its name. It is important to know that in the sixteenth century, Ghana became one of the Portuguese colonies, and because of its abundance of gold, it was named the Gold Coast. England occupied the coast in 1874 and invaded the entire territory in 1895. Also, it was from Ghana that hundreds of thousands of Africans were brought to the American continent to be sold as slaves.

The context of the story is that in the middle of 1925, Aggrey participated in a meeting of popular leaders who were discussing various methods for the liberation of Ghana from England. The opinions were divided, some choosing to rise up in arms, others opting for a more political approach, which later prevailed under the leadership of Kwame N'Krumah. Still others were contented with the colonization to which Africa had been subjected and were seduced by the English philosophy. This group was in favor of the English presence as a method of modernization and a way to be connected to a world considered modern and civilized.

Aggrey was paying close attention to each of the discourses presented by the leaders and realized that the most important leaders supported the English cause, disregarding the past, renouncing all the dreams of liberty. He then raised his hand and asked for the floor. Calmly and with all the patience of a wise man, he solemnly recounted the following story (also related in Boff 2002):

Once a peasant went into the neighboring woods to hunt for a bird that he could keep captive in his home. He was able to capture an eaglet, and he put him in his chicken coop along with all the chickens. The eaglet ate corn and everything else that the chickens would eat, even though the eagle was supposed to be the king/queen over all the other birds.

Five years later (an eaglet becomes an adult eagle in seventy-five to eighty days and has a life expectancy of thirty years), a naturalist came to the visit the peasant. As they walked through the garden, the naturalist observed the eagle and commented, "That bird there is not a chicken; it's an eagle." "I know it's an eagle," replied the peasant, "but it was raised as a chicken. It is no longer an eagle but has transformed itself into a chicken just like the others, even though its wings are almost three meters wide."

"It cannot be," replied the naturalist. "It is and forever will be an eagle. It has the heart of an eagle, and that heart will cause it to rise up and soar into the highest heavens one day." "No," insisted the peasant. "It has transformed itself into a chicken, and it will never again fly like an eagle."

Then the two decided upon a test. The naturalist took the eagle, raised it up high, and said, "Now that you have become an eagle, you belong in the sky and not on the earth. Spread your wings and fly." But to the naturalist's dismay, the eagle remained perched atop his arm, seemingly distracted by its surroundings. The eagle saw the chickens below, pecking around in the dirt, and joined them.

The peasant said, "I told you so. It has transformed itself into a simple chicken." The naturalist argued, "It is an eagle, and an eagle will always be an eagle. We will try again tomorrow." The next day, the naturalist ascended to the roof of the house with the eagle on his arm. Again he told the eagle, "Now that you have become an eagle, you belong in the sky and not on the earth. Spread your wings and fly." But again when the eagle saw the chickens on the ground, pecking around in the dirt, it jumped down to be with them.

Again the peasant smiled and told the naturalist, "As I said, it has transformed itself into a chicken." "No," the naturalist firmly replied. "Tomorrow we will try the test again, and tomorrow I will make him fly." The next day the peasant and the naturalist got up early in the morning and took the eagle out of the city, away from all the homes. They traveled to the high mountain peaks.

The naturalist lifted the eagle up high and ordered, "Eagle, now that you are a full-grown eagle, you belong in the sky and not on the ground. Spread your wings and fly!" The eagle looked at its surroundings and trembled as if it were experimenting with a new life, but it would not fly. Then the naturalist pointed the eagle in the direction of the sun so that it could behold the clarity the sunlight provided, as well as the wide expanse of the horizon.

In that moment, the eagle spread its powerful wings and let out the typical screech of an eagle: "Kau-kau!" It puffed itself up with pride, finally recognizing its sovereignty, and began to fly into the heavens. The eagle circled higher and higher each time until it could no longer be seen from the ground far below it.

Aggrey concluded, "Brothers, sisters, and compatriots, we were created in the image and likeness of God, but there have been some people who have made us think like chickens. Many of us have even begun to believe that we are, in fact, chickens, but we are eagles. For that reason, friends, we must spread our wings and fly. Let us fly like the eagles and never again be satisfied with just pecking around in the dirt."

Pastoral counselors, like the naturalist of Aggrey's story, are capable of seeing the potential, power, and strengths of people, and in the tradition of Jesus, they commit themselves to helping people fly toward wholeness. And like the naturalist, pastoral counselors need more than just the vocation to provide effective care of the soul. Today competent pastoral care and counseling includes the ability to work and function with a diverse and pluralistic society. Multicultural competence requires that pastors and religious leaders be informed about the different cultural factors influencing people's lives. The Latino/a population, as the largest minority and fastest-growing group in the United States of America, is certainly challenging spiritual caregivers to broaden their knowledge about culture and to become acquainted with other worldviews.

LATINO/AS:
DISTINCTIVE AND DIVERSE

The Latino/a population is a polyculture combining a heterogeneous and multicolored group of people who have diverse ethnicities, languages, religions, and socioeconomic and educational status yet maintain distinctive features and principles that make them "one" particular people.

This diversity requires spiritual caregivers to approach every Hispanic with an attitude of humility, keeping in mind that *Cada persona es un mundo* (Every person is a world). In addition, in the Latino/a population, there is not one unique way of doing things, because people are always becoming and constructing their own realities. Thus, to pretend to use a particular theological or counseling approach with the Latino/a people is illusionary in nature and deceptive in intent. *Creativity* is the word that comes to mind while working with Latino/a populations.

The study of the Latino/a community needs to be initiated by looking at the heart and centerpiece of the community: the family and religious rituals. Family—seen as a community of people connected by blood, adoption, marital agreement, and/or emotional links with a strong sense of togetherness—is the main source of support, care, guidance, and healing for the Latino/a people. For most Hispanics, the family is the place where they draw their strength, celebrate their achievements, lament their losses, perpetuate their values, and experience the fullness of what it means to be human. Indeed, it is in family where they triumph and fail, where they get sick, and where they get well.

As in any population, the Latino/a family is facing many psychosocial challenges and is increasingly becoming vulnerable and subject to marital disruptions, structural breakdowns, and erosion of values (Vega 1990). But historically the Hispanic family has used its resourceful, permeable, and adaptive characteristics to face difficult psycho-socio-economic trials with success. For that end, the Latino/a family has developed theories and strategies that merit our attention and study.

Latino/a people face family issues the same way they approach diseases of the body. As the disease appears, the entire family is mobilized and comes together to join forces, fight, and find meaning. *En la unión está la fuerza.* (There is power in togetherness.) If the family resources seem limited or insufficient to combat the "intruder and disruptive situation," the family solicits outside help. The "healer" approaches the family with respect for their values, traditions, and idiosyncrasies and, by building on the family resources, becomes an active part of the family. Then, in togetherness, they tackle the issues.

Faith and religion are present in most experiences of Latino/a people. The spiritual realm is consulted and used in issues related to life, education, health, economics, politics, family, and personal challenges. The religious phenomenon is so prevalent and pervasive that it is not seen as something you *have* but who you *are*. In this way, we are spiritual beings trying to be humans. The abundance of symbols and rituals with religious meanings used by Hispanics to connect with the Eternal One demonstrates the need of Latino/a people to transcend and live in harmony with the rest of creation.

Pastoral care and counseling work with Hispanics requires that spiritual caregivers be aware of the role of faith and family in people's pathos and healing process. In this context, "pastoral care and counseling" refers to the holistic service provided by God's representatives, who after having accepted the commitment of being agents of healing, choose to share God's grace and love. These pastoral caring actions are done with the intention to ensure the holistic well-being, or *shalom*, of God's people. Pastoral care and counseling is thus seen as a way of cooperating with God's work in the process of bringing into being the *imago dei* in each human being. Ismael Garcia (1997, 5) asserts, "Our dignity, and the respect due to us because of it, finds its ground in our being created in the image of God. Our intelligence, memory, imagination, freedom, and the capacity to transform our social and natural world are signs of our being creative agents that share in God's image and likeness."

1

BACKGROUND AND OVERVIEW OF THE LATINO/A CULTURE

Hispanics are a polyculture. This indicates a very heterogeneous and multicolor group of people with a combination of ethnicities, an array of languages, a variety of religions, and various socioeconomic and educational statuses (Vega 1990). Although diverse, a polyculture has distinctive features and principles that make its members one particular people.

Given this diversity, Latino/as defy simplistic explanations and categorization. They represent more than twenty countries and more than 580 million people living in South America, Central America, North America, the Caribbean, Europe, Asia, Africa, and Australia (Brea 2003). The majority of people of Latino/a heritage live in Latin America (520 million), which in this context refers to nations of Spanish, Portuguese, and indigenous languages located in South America, Central America, and the Caribbean (Brea 2003). Another 50 million live on the Iberian Peninsula. Cristina Torres (2001) of the World Health Organization estimates that 10.18 percent of the total Latin American population is Amerindian. The U.S. Census Bureau (2004) reports that as of July 1, 2003, there were 39.9 million Hispanics in the United States, representing 13.5 percent of the country's population (not including the 3.9 million Puerto Ricans living on that island). Two-thirds (66.9 percent) of these Hispanics are of Mexican origin, 14.3 percent are Central and South American, 8.6 percent are Puerto Rican, 3.7 percent are Cuban, and the remaining 6.5 percent are of other Hispanic origins. According to the Pew Hispanic Center (2004), 46 percent of the Latino/a population residing in the United States is bilingual (Spanish and English), 40 percent speak only Spanish, and 14 percent use English almost exclusively. The Latino/a or Hispanic people living in the United States of America are as multiethnic and pluralcultural as those living in Latin America.

This diversity invites pastoral caregivers to practice humility and recognize that the pathways to emotional, cognitive, relational, and spiritual healing among Hispanics are many, as

Cada persona es un mundo (Each person is a world in his or her own right). Thus, as we asserted in the introduction, it is illusionary and deceptive to suggest there is a single way of assisting people of Latino/a heritage. Although Latino/as share many worldviews and cultural factors, they remain a polyculture of men and women who believe that life is best lived when it is lived in togetherness and in community. Latino/as are genetically 99.9 percent similar to men and women across the planet, but that 0.1 percent matters greatly. It is in the best interest of culturally sensitive and competent pastoral caregivers to carefully consider that "little" difference.

HISPANIC ROOTS

A good place to begin describing Hispanics is to look at our roots: America. In the fifteenth century, Christopher Columbus (1451–1506) and his partners found many civilized societies that were well developed and highly structured with clear sociopolitical and technological practices revealing their wisdom and entrepreneurial spirits (Lockhart and Schwartz 1984; Fernandez-Armesto 2003). The inhabitants of these lands, who perhaps immigrated from Africa, Asia, and Australia about ten thousand years ago, were strategically established throughout South, Central, and North America as independent and autonomous societies with diverse cultural, religious, social, and family values. Many of these societies had great and well-developed cities, pyramids, empires, long-distance trade, roads, advanced agricultural techniques, and written codes of law. Although there were certain cultural similarities within the many inhabitants of these lands, these civilizations were diverse and independent of each other (Lockhart and Schwartz 1984).

The invader Columbus named this vast and diverse group of people Indians, as he thought he had arrived in Asia. This could indicate that being named by the dominant culture is not a new phenomenon. People eventually learned to deal with the naming and then reluctantly used that given name, as is also the case with the term *Hispanics*. The term *Hispanic* or *Latino/a*, although it makes sense from a political or marketing point of view, does not do justice to the diversity that characterizes the Latino/a people (Suarez-Orozco and Páez 2002).

Dominant cultures tend to name those they want to dominate. For instance, *Indians* was the name given by the Iberians to the dozens of civilizations that populated these two continents. The name *Indians* falsely gave the impression that the inhabitants of the Western Hemisphere were a united group of people, in contrast to the reality that they were culturally, economically, and politically diverse and had limited or no contact with the rest of humankind. Felipe Fernández-Armesto (2003) proposes that the notion of America as a homogenous and united hemisphere was the result of invaders' and exploiters' imagination to justify their enterprises and to make their task more manageable. Perhaps the same could be said for terms such as *Hispanics* or *Latino/as.*

The encounters between European, Amerindian, Asian, and African cultures gave origin to a unique group of people of white, Black, Amerindian, and mostly mestizo backgrounds who continuously strive to live harmoniously with nature, others, and self. This multicolor polyculture demands of pastoral caregivers humility in their attempt to understand the complexity of what it means to be Latino or Latina.

In summary, *Hispanics* refers to a pluriculture, multiethnic, mariachi, salsa, tutti-frutti mosaic of people who sound good, look exotic, taste great, move quick, and are found everywhere. The father-in-law of one author (Esteban) often says Hispanics are like the one-dollar bill: they are everywhere, and everybody likes them. The first part of this statement has some elements of truth, but the second half of that statement is far from being true, as discrimination continues to be rampant at both personal and institutional levels (Rivers and Morrow 1995; Comas-Diaz 2001; Montalvo 1991).

CHARACTERISTICS OF THE LATINO/A POLYCULTURE

As a multiethnic community, Latino/a or Hispanic people escape generalizations and categorical stereotypes. As Amerindians, Hispanics see no need to disregard, diminish, or eliminate the cultures they encounter in their path or pilgrimage. On the contrary, they are open to embracing aspects of other cultures to enrich their own. As multicultural beings, Latino/as understand there is no need to eliminate one cultural background in order to make space for the other; they affirm that many cultures might coexist and strengthen each other. Hispanics are one in the sense of service and goals, but many concerning customs, religions, color, socio-economic status, geography, and education.

At the heart of the Latino/a community is the family, the main source of support, care, guidance, and healing for the Latino/a people. There are as many types of families as there are Latino/as in the world. Family diversity implies that there is not a single model or pattern of family relationship that Hispanic families must follow to be functional and healthy. The idea is to treat or approach each Hispanic family with its idiosyncrasies and distinctiveness.

Traditional understanding of family therapy and counseling have been helpful in the sense that we now consider the impact not just of the internal psyche of an individual but also of the social and contextual influence for people's cognitive, affective, behavioral, and relational functioning. However, when pastoral caregivers and clinicians try to apply traditional theories and pastoral and family counseling approaches to multicultural families, the risk of harm is high, as many of these assumptions ignore the contextual and ecological family implications of clinical practice (Luepnitz 1988; Rogoff 2003). For instance, the notion of the family coming once a week for counseling for a determined number of sessions does not apply well to many Latino/a people. They might come for one session to complement the therapeutic work that is taking place through relatives, friends, *comadres, compadres* (godparents), and other social and health care professionals and then return weeks or months later for more consultation. This intermittent style of counseling and therapy has often been interpreted to mean the client is resistant or has an uncooperative spirit. However, it is important to remember that most Latino/as see therapy or counseling as a collaborative effort among clinician, self, relatives, and friends (Rojano 2004). The role of the pastoral counselor is not that of the "only expert" and protagonist, but that of a collaborator and companion traveler. Moreover, because of the idea of community, the life journey is a communal experience where several persons or a caravan of people are involved in the healing process.

Family diversity, with its structure, continues to be the cornerstone and the building block of the Hispanic community, society, and culture. For most Hispanics, the family is the place from which they draw their strengths, celebrate their achievements, lament their losses, perpetuate their values, learn and maintain their motivations, and experience the fullness of what it means to be human. Indeed, it is in family where they triumph and fail, where they get sick, and where they heal. In addition, the family is charged with the process of enculturation, as older members transmit the cultural knowledge, awareness, and skills into the next generations (Casas and Pytluck 1995).

Iberian, African, and Amerindian views of family relations have shaped the Latino/a or Hispanic understanding of family (Lockhart and Schwartz 1984). Iberians, highly influenced by the Roman Catholic Church and Islam, saw the father as the head of the house with the authority to make all decisions regarding the future of the family. The patriarch would run the family as a mini-estate where each member—wife, children, and servants—was expected to function, contribute, and work toward the well-being of the family unit or property.

Most Amerindian family members were interdependent, living and working together toward sustaining the community or tribe. The family, consisting of the father, mother, sons, daughters, close and distant relatives, along with other members of the household and tribe, was in charge of the education, care, discipline, and formation of the children. The flora, fauna, and cosmos were seen as part of the family that deserved respect and care. The elders of the tribe or community were in charge of passing the wisdom, culture, values, religion, art, music, and principles from one generation to the next. They used storytelling as the main medium to pass on that heritage. The kinship system defined the direction, ethos, responsibilities, administration, relationships, and future of the family.

Most Amerindian marriages served as an alliance between families, who decided to join efforts and strengths to better protect, educate, preserve, nurture, and guarantee the well-being of the community. Parents and elders of the community were the main people in charge of studying the history, physical health, personality, talents, and preferences of the future couples with the intention of finding the matching characteristics that would secure the success of the relationship.

In the African family, the mother, father, grandparents, siblings, relatives, close friends, and neighbors formed the network and kinship necessary for the appropriate development of family members.

This pattern was influential in shaping what we know today as the Latino/a family (Willie and Reddick 2003). The African American family includes qualities such as solidarity, cooperation, sharing, caring, cross-generational support, charity, awareness of the impact of oppression, sense of humor, respect, religiousness, and faith, all of which are common elements within Latino/a families. A large number of Blacks are Hispanics. For instance, in the Dominican Republic, 84 percent of the population is Black, Cuba is 62 percent Black, Brazil 46 percent, Colombia about 21 percent, Panama 14 percent, Venezuela more than 10 percent, Nicaragua over 9 percent, Ecuador more than 5 percent, and the rest of Latino/a countries between 1 and 4 percent Black (Torres 2001). For centuries, Blacks and Latino/as have mutually enlightened, supported, and developed each other.

Hispanic families are so diverse that it is difficult to speak of a typical Latino/a family. Like individuals, every family is a world in its own right. A contextual clinician and researcher will pay special attention to each family's peculiarity and level of cultural transition. The range of cultural exposure and cultural incorporation among Hispanic families varies from families with three hundred years of history in the United States to others who have just arrived from Latin American countries (Suarez-Orozco and Páez 2002). However, regardless of their time in the United States, many Latino/a families still face issues of discrimination, cultural racism, linguistic discrimination, isolation, racial profiling, and a crisis of belonging. In addition, undocumented Hispanic families face issues of distrust, denial of medical and educational access, and economic marginalization, among other difficulties (Lee 1999; Paniagua 2004).

Familismo, or the sense of loyalty, solidarity, cooperation, and interdependence, seems to be the cornerstone of most Latino/a families (Gloria and Peregoy 1996; Falicov 1996). It is common to hear from *tíos* and *tías* (uncles and aunts) this *dicho* (saying): *El que le pega a su familia se arruina,* denoting that family must be the priority and that under no circumstance is betrayal to the family encouraged. The idea that problems and conflicts belong and stay within the family is very much part of the Latino/a family's belief system.

This issue of loyalty, along with a healthy and necessary paranoia present in most Hispanic families, needs to be taken into consideration when working with them. Culturally sensitive clinicians keep this in mind at the beginning and throughout the therapeutic relationship. Clinicians do their best to establish an environment of safety, trust, respect, and reciprocity or *personalismo*, which will allow the family to feel *en casa* (at home) and that by consulting with a counselor they are not betraying the unwritten family code about loyalty, but seeking to strengthen the family relationship. Furthermore, multicultural, competent clinicians will be ready to process Latino/as' issues of guilt and shame resulting from their sharing their family issues with a stranger. Failure to address these issues may promote a premature termination of the therapeutic relationship.

ACCULTURATION OF LATINO/AS

We think of acculturation as the process of enriching one's culture and roots by incorporating many of the lifestyles and worldviews found within the culture encountered in a life journey. This mutual and reciprocal process of interchanging values, beliefs, customs, attitudes, and relationships becomes the cornerstone of growth, learning, development, and advancement. Latino/as seem reluctant to use the word *acculturation*, as it generally implies a discard of one's cultural roots in order to embrace the dominant culture. Perhaps this way of seeing acculturation reminds Latino/as of what the Iberians did in forcing Amerindians to abandon and destroy their worldviews and ways of connecting with themselves, others, nature, and divine beings.

Acculturation, according to John W. Berry (1997), refers to "integration." Some Hispanic families going through this period of integration may experience an array of emotions and stressful events that include a sense of alienation, psychosomatic symptoms, parenting confusion, identity issues, and interpersonal marital conflicts (Leyendecker and Lamb 1999; Flores et al. 2004). However, most Hispanic families—perhaps for their instinctual-indigenous openness to embrace other cultures—show no signs of distress in incorporating values, customs, and religious practices from other cultures (Moyerman and Forman 1992).

The four modes of acculturation suggested by Berry (1997)—assimilation, separation, marginalization, and integration—are an example of the difficulty in applying this social construct to the Latino/a population. Assimilation implies that individuals have to abandon, disengage, and mutilate their native cultures and values to adapt to those found in the dominant cultures (LaFromboise, Coleman, and Gerton 1993). In other words, you take all your cultural *ropaje* (clothing) and burn it or give it away to make space for the new culture. Separation refers to people retaining their cultural heritages and backgrounds but rejecting those of the majority culture (Berry 1997). The marginalization mode implies rejection of both "mother" and dominant culture. Berry's last mode, integration, suggests that people retain their ethnic culture but embrace many of the dominant culture's features.

ETHNIC IDENTITY

An ethnic identity results from the process of becoming aware of the impact of one's cultural roots (languages, beliefs, customs, nationality, gender, sexual orientation, age, religions, and socioeconomic status) on our ways of thinking, expressing emotions, acting, imagining, sensing, and relating. Hispanics appear reluctant to use the traditional racial division because the construct of race is of a political origin that is sometimes utilized to perpetuate discrimination and to promote competition and divisions among different groups (Gracia and De Greiff 2000). Instead, perhaps they prefer to use ethnic cultural identity, which recognizes personal and group differences but calls them to cultural cooperation and interdependence.

Developing this process of ethnic identity takes a lifetime, spanning from conception to death, as we are continuously learning about our cultural roots, the culture encountered, and their influences in our daily lives. The ways Latino/a families ethnically perceive themselves vary from person to person and from family to family. This life span experience cannot be boxed in stages or a hierarchical model because ethnic identity in Latino/a family members is fluid, contextual, permeable, and based more on social and cultural factors than on physical characteristics.

SPIRITUALITY AMONG HISPANICS

Hay de todo en la viña del Señor. (In the Lord's vineyard, there is a little of everything.) Faith and religion are present in most experiences of Latino/a people. The spiritual realm is consulted and used in issues related to life, education, health, economics, politics, family, and personal challenges. The religious phenomenon is so prevalent and pervasive that it is not seen as something that you have but who you are. In this way, we are spiritual beings trying to be humans. The abundance of symbols and rituals with religious meanings used by Hispanics to connect with the transcendent is a demonstration of the need of Latino/a peoples to live in harmony with nature, the universe, and self.

The polycultural nature of the Latino/a people is also seen in their diverse expressions of faith and its ways to connect with that which is transcendent. Perhaps for Hispanics the clearest way to understand their spirituality is to see its development as a syncretic religious practice that combines features of Amerindian, Christian, Islamic, Jewish, and African religions. The Roman Catholic faith was cautiously and overtly imposed, but native Amerindians and African slaves were still able to preserve their religious rituals and beliefs by incorporating them into the dominant Roman Catholic tradition. For instance, in Bolivia an Amerindian sculptor made two images of their ancient gods of nature and told the priest that these images were those of Saints Peter and Paul. Curiously, the number of attendants at the Sunday religious service increased remarkably (González 2003; Wiarda and Kline 2001).

Today, although less than 20 percent of Latino/as attend church regularly, the majority of them profess to ascribe to the Roman Catholic faith. A second large group consists of Latino/as who see themselves as spiritual people but maintain a level of suspicion of traditional faith groups such as the Roman Catholic and Evangelical movements. Some see the Roman Catholic Church at times as exploiting Latino/as and the Evangelical movement as an instrument of the North American empire. However, the Protestant and Evangelical faith tradition is increasingly becoming more popular with Hispanics, represented in Chile by 12 percent and in other countries, including Guatemala, as much as 25 to 35 percent of the population (Wiarda and Kline 2001). Other faith traditions include Muslim, Jewish, and Eastern religious practices. In summary, the Hispanic people value and treasure their spirituality, but this is as diverse as the culture itself.

Spirituality, religion, and faith are central to Latino/a families' survival and resilience. In practice, it is difficult to separate these conceptual constructs as they are seen as concrete attitudes, affective expressions, and actions that are read through the lenses of the community. The faith is lived within the context of the community. Respect and reverence for the transcendent, universe, nature, and neighbors are expressed through many rituals and symbols that vary from family to family. Therefore, religion, faith, and spirituality are intimately connected and better understood when seen as an undivided whole.

Spirituality is about relationship and intimacy with the transcendent, the self, and others. This web of relationships is what Latino/a families have historically used to face adversities, celebrate achievements, and make sense of their existence. The human being, seen as a social and holistic being with a body, mind, and spirit that are indissolubly connected and influencing each other, achieves wholeness within these three types of relationships. Culturally sensitive clinicians and researchers working with Latino/a families will understand that spirituality or connectedness is an integrated part of their daily functioning and that tending to the whole person within the community context is essential for the healing process.

COMMUNITY AND COLLECTIVISM

As social beings, Hispanics are relationship oriented. They exist in order to be in community. Hispanics are born, reproduce, grow, unfold, mature, and die in community. Because of their gregarious nature, they need the community in order to receive the healing power of relationships. Human interactions do not take place in isolation; rather, they occur in connection with others, self, and the transcendent. Pastoral counseling approaches with Hispanics must take place within the context of the community.

We know that persons cannot survive by themselves and that it is only in connection with others that it is possible to experience life to the fullest. In that direction, Judith V. Jordan (2000) asserts that the main thrust of human development is the movement toward mutuality and toward relatedness. She goes further to suggest that the source of most human suffering is disconnection and isolation. The cognitive, emotional, social, and spiritual healing occurs mainly in the presence of caring communities where love, sharing, interdependency, and cooperation characterize the interaction, where the clinicians and consultees join effort to make meaning of the experiences and embrace each other in the journey to wholeness.

Throughout history, particularly in European and North American cultures, there has been a tension between the individual and the community. Perhaps this friction is due in part to lack of balance in honoring and celebrating people's individual uniqueness, self-determination, and individual responsibility while at the same time acknowledging the importance and well-being of the community. A healthy and balanced approach calls for valuing the person's uniqueness and freedom while recognizing that the maximum human potential is experienced in relationships. This healthy approach emphasizes interdependency and cooperation rather than polarization and competition (Montilla 2005).

Most Latino/a people do not negate the value, respect, and dignity of each person but capitalize on the importance of coming together, caring for each other, and recognizing our needs for interdependency. They celebrate the reciprocal connection between the individual and community in which principles of equality, justice, and freedom are mutually respected. The idea is to value the uniqueness of each member of the community while keeping in mind the social responsibility of working together for the common good (Montilla 2004).

The meaning of community is illustrated in *Fuenteovejuna*, a play by Félix Lope de Vega. The story is about the small town named Fuenteovejuna, which is under the tyrannical rule of Don Fernán Gómez, Knight Commander of the Order of Calatrava. After much suffering, the townspeople finally rebel and kill the commander, placing his head on a pike as the banner of their freedom. Their battle cry is "*Fuenteovejuna, todos a una*" (Fuenteovejuna, all are one). When the Grand Master of the Order hears of this, he appeals to Ferdinand and Isabella, who appoint a judge-inquisitor to find the guilty parties and punish them.

The judge, however, finds that he can make little progress in his inquiry, for whenever he asks, "*¿Quién mató al comandante?*"

(Who killed the commander?), the answer is always the same: *"Fuenteovejuna, señor"* (Fuenteovejuna, my lord). Irritated, he tortures three hundred of the local inhabitants. Still, from all of them—men, women, children, and people in their old age—the answer is the same: *"Fuenteovejuna, señor."* Finally, the judge asks for instructions from Isabella and Ferdinand, who respond that, given such unanimity, there must have been just cause for the commander's death. González (1990) uses this metaphor to illustrate the essence of communal life, as the entire town realized that the community, not any individual in it, killed the commander. Likewise, if one member of a community is facing some emotional, cognitive, social, or spiritual challenge, the entire community joins in the hurting.

EMOTIONS FROM THE LATINO/A PERSPECTIVE

Latino/as are emotional beings who experience life as a whole. Indeed, they are emotional beings trying to be humans. Emotions are natural physiological responses to internal and external stimuli (Greenberg 2004) but read or interpreted through psychological and sociocultural lenses. The reading of these experiences through Hispanic eyes is very particular because the "Hispanic alphabet of emotions" has been composed with the help of Amerindians, Africans, and Iberians.

The emotions as a physiological phenomenon might be universal, but the ways of displaying them vary almost from family to family. Emotions are also symbols that can communicate love, care, disgust, or disapproval (Okun, Fried, and Okun 1999), as well as values and concerns. Expressions of happiness, sadness, surprise, fear, disgust, anger, and contempt might have some universal elements (Ekman and Friesen 1975), but the way they are uttered and used among Latino/as is very peculiar to each person. For instance, a person who is crying at a funeral might not be feeling sad, but rather he or she knows that within the culture, weeping conveys the idea of caring, so the person joins in the crying.

Most Hispanics would not refrain from expressing emotions, either negative or positive, in public because the idea of privacy seems to be less important than being transparent. Yet stereotyping Hispanics as *alborotados* (wild, roaring) is not prudent, because the person, cultural setting, and situation dictate to a great extent which and how emotions are conveyed. Social-related emotions such as shame (*verguenza*), guilt, indebtedness, *simpatia* (sympathy), and respect are encouraged in community-oriented societies (Matsumoto 1994).

RESPETO AND AUTHORITY

The "person in authority" within the Latino/a family (usually the maternal grandmother, oldest sister, or woman whom the family recognizes as an authority within the community) could be the most influential person in the decision-making process. She would encourage each family member, females and males, including children, to have a voice in the matter. It is very important for pastoral counselors working with Hispanics to be aware of the persons in a position of authority and leadership, because the failure or success of the pastoral intervention and therapeutic process will be highly shaped by the level of involvement of the group's "leader."

The healer or pastoral counselor will be most effective when she or he "becomes" a family member. This process of becoming part of the family starts with the establishment of a relationship that must be based on trust, truthfulness, respect, and reciprocity of thought, feelings, and relationship. This "joining" (Minuchin 1974) stimulates family members to engage in sharing their personal stories, their "living human webs" or network of support, their hopes and dreams. Because the healer or pastoral caregiver is not the single protagonist in the healing process, she or he welcomes the participation of the wider community to include perhaps educators, social workers, religious leaders, traditional healers, and medical personnel (Bronfenbrenner 1979).

Most importantly, the multiculturally competent and sensitive pastoral counselor must strive to connect and be present with each family member. Equality, power sharing, compassion, availability, and love characterize this connection and relational experience. Gabriel Marcel (1950) suggests that being present is a gift of grace in which two or more human beings engage in self-sharing and mutual availability. The implication of this way of being present is that healers dispose of themselves to be completely connected with the other, which in turn will facilitate "the discovery of depth through togetherness" (Marcel 1950).

2

THE PASTORAL CAREGIVER AS PERSON

Pastoral counseling is a relational and clinical encounter between two or more human beings who accept the premise that wholeness is possible when the spiritual, emotional, physical, and social dimensions are considered within a framework of communal living. The healing impact of the encounter hinges on the connection that arises as a result of addressing each other with respect and mutuality within an atmosphere of trust, nourishing spirit, empowering dialogues, and hopeful interchanges. This is the connotation of *pastoral*, a word that comes to us from the Latin *pascere*, which could be translated as to nourish or to feed. The word *counseling* is connected to the Latin words *consilium/consulere*, which implies community or coming together to gain wisdom and support.

In this context, pastoral counseling is not the exclusive "belonging" or property of professional religious leaders, but the tool that people of faith use to discuss their hopes, pains, dreams, and concerns about life and world, as well as to make meaning of their existence. However, members of the community, recognizing the importance of these healing and empowering dialogues, may seek professional training to become more effective "healers" or pastoral counselors. The preparation may consist of extensive theological and counseling training that equips people with attitudes, skills, and knowledge within the field to provide efficient, competent, and professional pastoral counseling services.

The attitude is listed first because the most important tool in helping others to become is not the technique but the person of the pastoral counselor. The central elements of the therapeutic and counseling relationship are the pastoral caregiver's human qualities, such as warmth, empathy, intelligent sympathy, genuine interest, and love for others (Boisen 1936). Current research is confirming that the person, in conjunction with the quality of the relationship, highly influences the positive outcome of the therapeutic connection and is a better predictor of a successful counseling intervention than the approach used to help the consultee (Luborsky et al. 1999; Lambert 1986; Herman 1993; Beutler et al. 2004).

That is why we believe that a member of the community of faith who wants to pursue training in pastoral counseling needs to start by exploring her or his life in relationship to the self, others, and the Eternal One. Because of the complexity of our human nature, this journey of discovery is not an easy and effortless pilgrimage.

HUMAN NATURE

We are complex, holistic, and biological beings who behave, emote, sense, imagine, think, and interact with one another in diverse and unpredictable ways (Lazarus 2000). Each one of us is an indissoluble unity and an indivisible whole where body, mind, and spirit move and work together with the intention of living harmoniously and in relationship. These interconnected dimensions represent different aspects of the same person, but they are not different substances or entities capable of functioning independently (González 1990).

The spiritual dimension of the person represents the entirety of one's being and serves as the anchor that unifies one's psychological, physiological, and sociological dimensions (Tournier 1964). It allows the person to experience and understand the reality of existence within the context of intimacy with self, others, and that which transcends usual limits. Indeed, we are spiritual beings trying to be humans.

We are created in the image of God with a voice, power, and an extraordinary capacity to relate (Langberg 1997). We are created in God's image to live as a community of men and women of faith and hope who celebrate the honor of being humans. "Again, the kingdom of heaven is like a merchant looking for fine pearls. When he found one of great value, he went away and sold everything he had and bought it" (Matthew 13:45-46, NIV). We read this parable as God seeking, finding, and reclaiming us. We see God as the Merchant expressing His great love, value, and desire to live in communion with us. The pearls of great price represent us as God's children who seem hidden in the world's confusion but with an immeasurable value and dignity.

Therefore, when God finds us, we might appear to be covered by dust, in a rough, rudimentary form, and without a clear shape.

However, God sees each person's potential and richness, the true value, the incalculable beauty, and the capacity to grow and be transformed, as well as the capacity to be a cocreator with God. In the words of poet Maya Angelou (1994, 73), we came "from the Creator like everyone else, trailing wisps of glory." The worth of each person is so great that God goes and sells everything in order to have us.

The Creator of the universe, the Sustainer of so many billions of galaxies, is willing to reach out to us, to reconcile and bring us into harmony with God's self. God put aside everything and became like one of us (Philippians 2:7). The act of giving up and selling everything that the Merchant had is the epitome of love and trust in the human being, the pearl of great price.

God reaches out to claim and reconcile us and to complete the work in us. And although the pearl of great price holds inner beauty, the outer layer appears rather ordinary. To make us whole, to make our true beauty visible, the Merchant with kindness, tenderness, gentle touch, and loving attitude began the process of polishing, shaping, and bringing out the inherent beauty of each human being.

God, the Jeweler, uses many tools to accomplish the task. The most important tool is the modeling God did for us through the life and ministry of Jesus Christ. In addition to this, God may use nature, family, special revelation, and formal and informal education. We believe pastoral counseling is a way to cooperate with God's work in the process of bringing out the *imago dei* in each human being. In the words of Leroy Howe (1995, 17), "That indestructible image makes possible an indissoluble fellowship with God and with all of creation as grace triumphs over judgment, reconciliation over condemnation, and life over death. The ultimate goal of all pastoral counseling is to help distressed persons discover anew and cherish this divine image within themselves and others, and by so doing, to experience life in all its fullness."

We see the pastoral counseling experience as a way to polish away cognitive, emotional, theological, and behavioral dust that blocks access to our own beautiful intimacy with God and other valuable "pearls." In fact, we believe that the ultimate goal of the pastoral counseling relationship is to restore the *imago dei* and to cooperate with the divine purpose, as "God's co-workers" (1 Corinthians 3:9, NIV).

CHARACTERISTICS OF A SENSITIVE AND COMPETENT PASTORAL COUNSELOR

As human beings created in the image of God with the capacity to love, to listen, to communicate, and to transform and be transformed, we inherently have what it takes to connect with others in meaningful and helpful ways. These innate attributes and life-enhancing talents can be enriched with formal or informal training in counseling and contextual theology. Pastoral counselors who desire to be more efficient and culturally competent invest time in enhancing their God-given abilities, exploring their attitudes, and acquiring a substantial body of knowledge within the field. Intentional and professional pastoral counselors need to develop skills to help people explore their thoughts, emotions, and relational styles, as well as to help them understand their issues and act in the light of their faith. Here is a list describing competent and efficient pastoral counselors:

- Competent pastoral counselors recognize that God is the ultimate source of healing and wholeness (Exodus 15:26; Psalm 147:3). Therefore, as instruments of healing, they remain connected with God as the source of power and saving grace.
- Competent pastoral counselors understand that love is the conduit for God's healing power and human transformation. They listen, speak, relate, and act in love toward the persons they serve (1 John 4:8; Leviticus 19:18; 1 Corinthians 16:14; Galatians 5:13; Witmer and Sweeney 1992).
- Competent pastoral counselors believe that everyone has equal access to God's power and transforming grace through the Spirit of God (John 14:26). They trust in people's capacity to transform themselves and their surroundings (Combs 1986).
- Competent pastoral counselors are aware of their power, authority, and limitations. They have a positive belief in self-in-relation and are aware that they are wounded healers and instruments of God's love (Romans 12:3, 16). They celebrate their self-efficacy but understand that they also are becoming and willing to be transformed by the relationship and stories of their consultees (Hebrews 5:2-3; Romans 1:11-12; Buber 1999).

- Competent pastoral counselors respect and believe that human beings were created in the image of God with the capacity to choose, grow, and create their own destiny and realities (Genesis 1:26). They respect people's freedom and encourage their holistic development.
- Competent pastoral counselors have a genuine interest in people's well-being and use all their resources to provide an environment and milieu where people's potential can unfold and move toward wholeness (John 21:15-19; Philippians 2:4; Romans 12:13; Cormier and Hackney 2005).
- Competent pastoral counselors are able to convey empathy accurately and to express and communicate compassion (Romans 12:15; John 11:33, 35, 36; Zechariah 7:9; Ephesians 4:32; Rogers 1957; Herman 1993).
- Competent pastoral counselors believe consultees have an active part in the healing process (Luke 18:42).
- Competent pastoral counselors are acquainted with uncertainty and mystery, and they resist temptation to resolve it rather than experience it (John 11:7-9). They recognize that life is complex and full of mysteries and that many of these ambiguities are impenetrable. Moore (1992) encourages pastoral counselors to accept the invitation to appreciate the puzzles, paradoxes, mysteries, and uncertainties of life and the world (Pietrofesa et al. 1978).
- Competent pastoral counselors listen to thoughts, emotions, behaviors, and patterns of relation attentively, without judging or condemning and with contextual understanding (James 1:19; Proverbs 18:13; Egan 2002).
- Competent pastoral counselors are aware of the consultee's strengths, motivations, and personal needs, and as clinician they resist the temptation to use their consultee's space and time to satisfy their own needs. They respect and trust the integrity of the therapeutic process.
- Competent pastoral counselors are connected with counseling and theological professional associations for collegiality and accountability and are willing to consult with colleagues and other professionals (Proverbs 15:22).
- Competent pastoral counselors recognize the importance of listening, attending, and accepting people, but at the same

time, they are clear that they have a prophetic role as pastoral
caregivers. They are willing to caringly confront consultees'
irrational expectations, cognitive distortions, self-destructive
and self-defeating behaviors, and conflictive patterns of relation (Romans 12:2).

- Competent pastoral counselors know that human beings are
  involved in an ongoing process of renovation and transformation (2 Corinthians 4:16). This renewing and internal experience is the result of the work of the Spirit in conjunction with
  people desiring to reflect God's character (Matthew 13:33;
  Philippians 1:6; 1 Thessalonians 5:14).
- Competent pastoral counselors are aware of their own humanity and vulnerabilities, and they wisely use self-revelation to
  connect with their consultees (2 Corinthians 2:4).
- Competent pastoral counselors have a healthy and respectful
  sense of humor (Proverbs 17:22).
- Competent pastoral counselors recognize that they are fallible
  human beings. They are willing to admit when they commit
  mistakes in the counseling process and are ready to apologize
  to their consultees.
- Competent pastoral counselors are friendly and practice hospitality (1 Peter 3:8-9).
- Competent pastoral counselors are ethical beings who are
  aware of their values, principles, and beliefs and resist temptation to impose them on their consultees.
- Competent pastoral counselors understand the importance
  of keeping confidentiality, and they do whatever is possible
  to guard professional secrecy. They know that breaking confidentiality can damage the consultee, the profession, and society in general.
- Competent pastoral counselors are aware of their prejudices and
  biases, and they avoid discriminating against people because of
  color, age, sex, gender, lifestyle, political affiliation, religious
  beliefs, ethnicity, social and marital status, and education.

3

A BIBLICAL MODEL OF PASTORAL CARE AND COUNSELING

Latino/as tend to read the Bible from a marginal and peripheral perspective (González 1992; De La Torre 2003). This manner of reading seems to be more liberating and empowering. Jesus invited his disciples to see the Word from the margins. He constantly taught his disciples that in order to be part of his reign, they needed to understand and experience life and the world through the eyes of the marginalized: women, eunuchs, children, poor, slaves, and physically handicapped (Matthew 19-20).

In Jesus' time, women were not even considered important enough to be counted in the census. They were essentially nonexistent, the property of the men. But Jesus said women are entitled to the same rights as men, not just in the context of divorce but in all areas. Therefore, if you want to be part of God's reign, see life through the eyes of women.

Another interesting component of the ministry from the margins is Jesus' take on eunuchs. Eunuchs were shunned by society. Some of them looked like women. In fact, it was often difficult to tell they were males. They were seen with such derision that they were not allowed into the temples, nor permitted to own a Bible or receive biblical teaching from the rabbis. They were among the lowliest of the low, outcasts. Therefore, if you want to be part of God's reign, see life through the eyes of the eunuchs.

Children also were considered insignificant and valueless. They, as the women, were not counted and were considered property. Jesus' disciples' attitudes toward children were consistent with that time period: they saw children as nuisances. Therefore, if you want to be part of God's reign, see life through the eyes of children.

The same can be said for the poor, the slaves, and the blind and physically handicapped. This entire population was on the fringes of society. These people were outside the mainstream of the social order and thus were generally ignored, shunned, or disregarded as being "less than." Jesus worked to break down barriers, was sensitive to their plight, and treated them with respect and dignity, something we all can strive to do in our ministry.

It is imperative that as pastoral caregivers we see God's reign from the perspective of the marginalized, those people on the periphery who often have no opportunity to give voice to their hearts' desires. We must give them a voice and a representation, as well as encouragement to draw upon their own God-given power and strength to grow into the promise of God's reign here on earth.

The traditional reading through the eyes of the powerful could be oppressive. The ones in power read and interpret the Bible to tell others, those on the periphery who historically have no power, what is right and what is wrong. This attitude assumes that those who live at the margins do not have the wherewithal to make their own decisions concerning right and wrong, and therefore must be told! The possibility of internal locus of control for those on the periphery is then not considered. This reading from the center is a way to ensure that the power remains with the ones doing the interpretation.

In the traditional reading, theology is seen as the study of God. This seems to be an arrogant assumption. How we can study God? How can we assume to know what God is? How can we pretend to study the Creator of this vast universe of more than one hundred billion galaxies? For us, theology is the dialogue human beings have about God and God's relationship with us and the rest of creation. This dialogue is dynamic, fluid, functional, contextual, and liberating.

To illustrate this type of dialogue and reading, we will use the model of pastoral counseling suggested by Isidor Baumgartner (1997). He exemplifies this method through the reading of Luke 24:13-35, which he separates into four sections: (1) *koinonia*, that is, to come close and accompany; to go beside the one who is on a journey; to accept one another; (2) *diakonia*, meaning to question and serve with empathy; to be still and quiet; (3) *martyria*, to interpret the word of God; to enlighten and discover the essence of the Scriptures; and (4) *liturgia*, the breaking of bread, prayer, and handling the symbols of the faith.

LIFE: A JOURNEY, A WALK TOWARD TRANSFORMATION

Now that same day two of them were going to a village called Emmaus, about seven miles from Jerusalem.

—Luke 24:13 (NIV)

Life seems more enjoyable when seen as a journey where the most important part is not arriving but the trip itself. Traditional reading of the Bible keeps inviting us to concentrate on the "mansions and streets of gold of the New Jerusalem," while disregarding the reality of today. It is true that we are voyagers, nomads, and travelers who move toward wholeness and deeper experiences with God, but we truly live our lives here and now. We understand that God's reign is a way of living more than a place where we are going. Today we can have abundant life where justice and love prevail, and with God's help, we construct our future, our *mañana*.

The God who lives in communion with himself and his creation is with us. God is with the oppressed, marginalized, and poor (Deuteronomy 10:18-19; Psalms 9:7-9; Proverbs 22:22-23). God's dream, which God has had since the foundation of the world, was to become human. God became one of us, mainly to be in communion with humankind and to make reconciliation and salvation accessible and real, as well as to give us a model for living.

God's presence is continuous and dependable. However, in some types of crises, it is difficult to feel God's abiding company. Perhaps the mourners and grievers on their way to Emmaus were asking how, in time of trouble, they should maintain their faith and sense of hope. "That same day two of them were on the way to Emmaus" (Luke 24:13, BLS). This journey was probably one of the most difficult they would ever take. They were going home surprised, disillusioned, sad, rejected, hopeless, angry, confused, and feeling abandoned by the God whom they followed. They felt empty and in a state of emotional and spiritual chaos. How many times did the prophets and apostles feel the same way these travelers felt? How many times have we felt like that?

These two travelers had lost their teacher, friend, companion, and above all, their Messiah who had come to free them from the oppression of sin and wickedness. They were undoubtedly going through severe hurt and sorrow. However, we can deduce that they were handling the hurt in a healthy way, since they were already on their way. This may mean that they were already dealing with their sorrow. "They were talking about all the things that had happened" (Luke 24:14).

KOINONIA

God comes beside us, keeps us company, and walks with us

As they talked and discussed these things with each other, Jesus himself came up and walked along with them.
—Luke 24:15 (NIV), emphasis added

We human beings have been created to live in community. It is in community where we experience life to its fullest, and it is in community where we better encounter pain and sorrow. These two disciples were sharing their pain by talking over what had happened. *"It so happened as they discussed and talked among themselves,* that Jesus Himself came to them as a stranger and walked along with them" (Luke 24:15, BLS, italics added). The Lord Jesus presented himself as a stranger who wanted to share their sorrow and walk along with them in the direction they were going. The Lord did not come to them with the intention of guiding them or changing their direction, but to accompany them.

To come near to another human being implies accepting that person just as he or she is. This means we have to overcome the temptation to want to clone or reproduce the way we think, imagine, act, and feel. "So then, accept each other mutually, just as Christ accepted you for the glory of God" (Romans 15:7).

To come near also implies placing oneself at the same level as the other person, assuming our part as sufferers, as wounded healers, and acknowledging our own fears, blindness, and limitations. Baumgartner (1997) comments that the person who in meeting God has experienced support and acceptance of his or her imperfections and has learned to accept him- or herself can also accept the dark side of others. "Every high priest is selected from among men and is appointed to represent them in matters related to God, to offer gifts and sacrifices for sins. He is able to deal gently with those who are ignorant and are going astray, since he himself is subject to weakness. This is why he has to offer sacrifices for his own sins, as well as for the sins of the people" (Hebrews 5:1-3, NIV).

This transparency and human permeability promotes God's saving and healing ambience. In this way we become agents of love, grace, and God's truth. "In everything set them an example by doing what is good. In your teaching show integrity, seriousness and soundness of speech that cannot be condemned, so that those who oppose you may be ashamed because they have nothing bad to say about us" (Titus 2:7-8, NIV).

It is good to keep in mind that the pastoral care service we offer is reciprocal. Each person we meet may be the door God uses to show us God's love, grace, and transforming power. The apostle Paul recognizes mutual caring when he writes, "I long to see you so that I may impart to you some spiritual gift to make you strong— that is, that you and I may be mutually encouraged by each other's faith" (Romans 1:11-12, NIV).

As fellow travelers and partners on the road of life, we and those who seek our help influence each other in the process of reaching the necessary level of maturity and wholeness. Hermann Hesse (1943/1982), in his novel *Magister Ludi* (also known as *The Glass Bead Game*), tells a tale that involves two renowned healers, Joseph and Dion, who lived in biblical times. These two healers were highly effective and used two different approaches to healing. The younger healer, Joseph, healed through quiet, calm presence, compassion, and reflective listening. He was very effective in treating people suffering from physical and emotional illnesses. Sufferers who came to him left his place feeling good about themselves, knowing that they were heard and understood. The older healer, Dion, used a confrontational and very directive approach. He was a great judge, chastiser, scolder, and rectifier. He treated those who came seeking help like children. He gave advice, punished by assigning penance, ordered pilgrimages, and compelled enemies to make up.

The two healers never met, and they worked as rivals for many years until Joseph grew spiritually ill, fell into dark despair, and was assailed with ideas of self-destruction. Recognizing his unstable emotional situation, he set out on a journey to the south to seek help from Dion. On his pilgrimage, Joseph rested one evening at an oasis, where he entered into a conversation with an older traveler. When Joseph described the purpose and destination of his pilgrimage, the traveler revealed his identity to Joseph. The older traveler was Dion himself.

Without hesitation Dion invited his younger, despairing rival into his home, where they lived and worked together for many years. Dion first asked Joseph to be a servant. Later he elevated him to a student and, finally, to a colleague holding equal status.

Years later, Dion became ill. On his deathbed, he summoned his younger colleague to hear his confession. Dion began to relate to Joseph about the time they met each other and how Joseph felt that it was a miracle that his fellow traveler was the healer from whom he was seeking help. Now that Dion was dying, he thought it necessary to break the silence about that miracle and to tell the truth. Dion confessed that about the same time Joseph was feeling sick, Dion also had fallen into despair and felt empty, spiritually dead, and unable to help himself. So, when they met at the oasis, Dion himself was on a journey to seek help; he was on a pilgrimage to a famous healer named Joseph. Irvin Yalom (2003) uses this story to illustrate the mutuality of care and reciprocity of healing.

Abraham Joshua Heschel (1976) presents to us the idea of a God in search of humans. It is difficult to understand the interest and care for humans that a Creator of a universe with billions of galaxies has for us. A living God who accompanies us during sadness, sorrow, and joy is a constant in the story of the nation of Israel:

> "I am the God of your father, the God of Abraham, the God of Isaac and the God of Jacob." . . . The Lord said, "I have indeed seen the misery of my people in Egypt. I have heard them crying out because of their slave drivers, and I am concerned about their suffering. So I have come down to rescue them from the hand of the Egyptians and to bring them up out of that land into a good and spacious land, a land flowing with milk and honey." (Exodus 3:6-8, NIV)

From the beginning, we find the Living God seeking human beings: "But the Lord God called to the man, 'Where are you?'" (Genesis 3:9, NIV). God looks for us to restore us, not to hurt us. Throughout the Holy Scriptures, God consistently takes the initiative of coming to meet the human being. This seeking, motivated by God's love and desire to restore communion with us, is a unique characteristic of our God, "who raises the fallen and supports the suffering" (Psalm 145:14, NIV). God was not satisfied with living amidst his people in the form of symbols, but completed his divine plan of becoming human: "And the Word became flesh and lived among us" (John 1:14, NIV). This is the maximum demonstration of what it means to come near and to accompany.

God is faithful and is with us in good and bad times: "The one who calls you is faithful and he will do it" (1 Thessalonians 5:24, NIV). Even "if we are faithless, He will remain faithful, for he cannot disown himself" (2 Timothy 2:13, NIV). Emmanuel, the Living God who suffers, cries, feels, and laughs with us, is a God who is faithful to the divine covenant. This sense of security we have in our Faithful Companion reflects what the psalmist says: "Even though I walk through the valley of the shadow of death, I will fear no evil, for you are with me; your rod and your staff, they comfort me" (Psalm 23:4, NIV). His promise is, "Surely I am with you always, to the very end of the age" (Matthew 28:20, NIV).

God comes near but is not necessarily visible

But they were kept from recognizing him.
—Luke 24:16

God has promised us his companionship and continued care in the course of our life on this world. This sense of companionship is more easily appreciated when we are not in crisis. However, when we are facing difficult situations and feel sunk, with no way out, it is often hard to feel God's presence. In fact, in crisis our capacity to reason is reduced, and our decision-making mechanism becomes cloudy. The truth is that our Creator, perhaps in an obscure, quiet, and unknown way, is beside us in our happiest as well as the most difficult moments of our lives. What happens is that we are blinded during moments of crisis.

When Guiezi, servant of the prophet Elisha, was confronted with a crisis, he was overcome with fear and could not see or feel God's presence:

> When the servant of the man of God got up and went out early the
> next morning, an army with horses and chariots had surrounded

the city. "Oh, my lord, what shall we do?" the servant asked. "Don't be afraid," the prophet answered. "Those who are with us are more than those who are with them." And Elisha prayed, "O Lord, open his eyes so he may see." Then the Lord opened the servant's eyes, and he looked and saw the hills full of horses and chariots of fire all around Elisha. (2 Kings 6:15-17, NIV)

Let us pray for the ability to see with the eyes of the heart in order to see how God accompanies us in the most difficult moments of our life.

Our God, Creator and Sustainer of the universe, takes care of you and me. The apostle Paul, speaking to the Athenians, confirms this truth: "God did this so that men would seek Him and perhaps reach out for Him and find Him, though He is not far from each one of us. 'For in him we live and move and have our being.' As some of your own poets have said, 'We are his offspring'" (Acts 17:27-28, NIV).

DIAKONIA

The God who accompanies us formulates questions for the purpose of restoration

He asked them, "What are you discussing together as you walk along?"
—Luke 24:17a (NIV)

From the beginning of human history, the formulation of questions has been a part of the communication and relationship between humans. The great inventions and advances had their beginning in an appropriately formulated question at the right moment. Through the ages and in all cultures, the most outstanding teachers in different areas of knowledge have used the question in the process of helping themselves and their students. For them, a good question is much more important than its answer. It is clear that the manner, style, and type of question formulated determine the effect that it will have.

Good questions, be they expressive, silent, or internal, can lead to reflection, self-study, creativity, and transformation. In contrast, questions made in an inappropriate way have the capacity to destroy and paralyze. Therefore, learning to formulate appropriate questions is not only important but also can make a difference between helping someone to grow or sinking a person into an emotional and spiritual quagmire.

From the very beginning, the Bible presents a God who asks questions:

"Where are you?" (Genesis 3:9)
"Where is your brother?" (Genesis 4:9)
"Where were you when I established the earth?" (Job 38:4)
"Who has believed our announcement?" (Isaiah 53:1)
"Who do you say that I am?" (Matthew 16:15)

The God who questions is also a God who accompanies and actively listens:

"What are you discussing on the way?" (Luke 24:17)
"What has happened?" (Luke 24:17, 19)

The Lord Jesus Christ made himself a part of the conversation as he formulated an open-ended question that led them to reflect, not just share information. This type of question has an incalculable therapeutic value, because its intent is not to fulfill a curiosity. On the contrary, it gives individuals the opportunity to use their mental and emotional capacity to evaluate the situation they face. This type of question communicates to persons the idea that they have the freedom to launch themselves in their own pain with the security that Jesus will accompany them.

The accompanying God listens actively and quietly

They stood still, their faces downcast.

—Luke 24:17b (NIV)

To answer a major question, we have to pause and consider the implications of the crisis before us. This process of pausing may be painful, but it is through this that we can start to see light and hope. We need to overcome the temptation to minimize the pain of others and instead stay with them while they process their emotions and express their sorrows. "When others are happy, be happy with them, and when they are sad, be sad" (Romans 12:15, CEV). At times we are premature in wanting people to see the light while they see only darkness. We need to put aside clichés like "Don't worry; everything is going to be all right," or "Cheer up—don't be so pessimistic." The best we can do at these times is to walk alongside them in that dark corridor, hand in hand.

The two travelers to Emmaus paused and were quiet, downtrodden, and very sad. In quiet times such as these, we can experience the transforming grace of God.

The two travelers, reflecting over what had happened, started to process their hurt by expressing their disillusionment. They said, "We had hoped that he was the one who was going to redeem Israel" (Luke 24:21, NIV). In other words, their expectations were tumbling down. They saw no future, felt like failures, and saw no way out. Feeling this way may be the first step toward healing and experiencing the grace and mercy of our God. This "Calvary" experience is a prerequisite to being able to experience the glory and transformation that await us. The apostle Paul presents it like this: "What you sow does not come to life unless it dies" (1 Corinthians 15:36, NIV).

MARTYRIA

God interprets and enlightens his Word

And beginning with Moses and all the Prophets, he explained to them what was said in all the Scriptures concerning himself.
—Luke 24:27 (NIV)

The Holy Scriptures have a restoring and saving power that goes beyond human understanding but that has concrete results. The author of the book of Hebrews confirms this power when he says, "For the word of God is living and active. Sharper than any double-edged sword, it penetrates even to dividing soul and spirit, joints and marrow; it judges the thoughts and attitudes of the heart" (Hebrews 4:12, NIV).

Scientific studies, anecdotes, and testimonies of people who have received complete healing through the reading of the Holy Scriptures clearly show the role they have in the healing process. To these people, the Bible is not a dry or dead text or a mere literary piece, but more than that, it is the Word of the Living God. In this context, when the person really listens to or reads the Bible stories, that person becomes a part of them. For example, in a study made with 101 patients suffering from cancer and 45 fathers and mothers of children with cancer, it was realized that visits by chaplains and pastoral counselors were effective and beneficial when they included, in their services, the reading of God's word (Larson and Larson, 1994).

A way to experience the healing power of the Holy Scriptures is to come to the reading with an attitude of respect, humility, and openness, allowing the Bible to speak to us as we are. In this way, we let the story or biblical text permeate and influence the way we think of God, life, and ourselves. The fact is that the stories we find in the Bible are very similar to the stories in our own lives. This allows us to feel and experience our own story in the light of the gospel of salvation and hope. In this way, our story is woven and mixed with the stories revealed in the Scriptures, where we derive the restorative and transforming powers that they contain.

Our nature and cultural inheritance, in some way, have conditioned us to respond positively to the stories. Fathers and mothers from the dawn of human history have found the usefulness of stories as vehicles for teaching, mental development, and social and spiritual development of boys and girls: "Impress them on your children. Talk about them when you sit at home and when you walk along the road, when you lie down and when you get up" (Deuteronomy 6:7, NIV). Our Lord Jesus Christ, knowing our nature, consistently used stories to relate his truth and explain his kingdom.

It is important to keep in mind that there are certain harmful ways of using the Bible that may lead to strengthening certain destructive and self-destructive behavior that people exhibit or adopt. There may be times when people use the Holy Scriptures as a defense mechanism or an instrument for ignoring certain subjects or internal conflicts they may be facing. To avoid these problems, we have to allow God's word to read us and transform us. If we approach the Bible with an open heart and under the direction of the Holy Spirit, we can receive the balm, the divine support, and thus drink from the fountain of life.

Once we accompany people in their pain and difficulties, we can lovingly and prophetically confront illogical thinking and irrational beliefs that may keep a person stagnant. "How reluctant you are to believe all that the prophets have spoken! Did not Christ have to suffer these things before entering His glory?" (Luke 24:25-26). Notice that these two disciples were not defensive but attentively listened to the words that the accompanying stranger had for them. In fact, they were so interested that they did not want to let him go and, even more, they persuaded him to sup with them: "But they urged him strongly, 'Stay with us, for it is nearly evening; the day is almost over.' So He went in to stay with them" (Luke 24:29 NIV).

Later on they confessed what was happening inside of them, saying, "Did not our hearts burn as He spoke with us on the road and explained the scriptures? (Luke 24:31 NIV). This happened because Jesus waited for the right moment to greet them with his love. Notice also that Jesus Christ used something that was common to them, the stories of faith found in the Holy Scriptures, to show them that there was something else, something they had not seen but that was available: freedom and a way out through him. "Then, beginning with Moses and the prophets, he explained the references made of Him in the Holy Scriptures" (Luke 24:27).

LITURGIA

The accompanying God reveals his identity by breaking bread

> *Then their eyes were opened and they recognized him, and he disappeared from their sight. . . . They got up and returned at once to Jerusalem. There they found the Eleven and those with them, assembled together.*
>
> *—Luke 24:31-33 NIV*

The symbols of faith are an invitation to participate in the mysteries of God. These symbols defy the traditional way we use reason, logic, and language. Symbols are something we can see here and now, but at the same time, they can transport us to the past as well as toward the future. The way the symbols of our faith work may, perhaps, escape our reasoning. However, what is sure is that these symbols have a powerful meaning to us, since it penetrates the innermost chambers of our being. Even if we do not understand the "how" of the symbols of faith, we do appreciate the quiet way in which our God reveals himself through the symbols.

The symbols of faith come together and thread our reality into the reality of God. This deep and mysterious reality may be hidden and has to be deciphered, or decoded, by us through the influence of the Holy Spirit. The apostle Paul says that only in the presence of the Holy Spirit do we really come to know God and ourselves:

> However, as it is written: "No eye has seen, no ear has heard, no mind has conceived what God has prepared for those who love Him" but God has revealed it to us by His Spirit. The Spirit searches all things, even the deep things of God. For who among men knows the thoughts of a man except the man's spirit within him? In the same way no one knows the thoughts of God except the Spirit of God. We have not received the spirit of the world but the Spirit who is from God, that we may understand what God has freely given us. This is what we speak, not in words taught to us by human wisdom but in words taught by the Spirit, expressing spiritual truths in spiritual words. The man without the Spirit does not accept the things that come from the Spirit of God, for they are foolishness to him, and he cannot understand them, because they are spiritually discerned. The spiritual man makes judgments about all things, but he himself is not subject to any man's judgment: "For who has known the mind of the Lord that he may instruct him?" But we have the mind of Christ (1 Corinthians 2:9-24, NIV)

The word *companion*, or one who accompanies, is a word made up of two Latin roots: *com* (to be with) and *panis* (bread). With this in mind, the translation of the word *companion* would be something like "someone with whom you share bread." The companion who drew near to these two travelers shared real and symbolic bread. In the words of Baumgartner (1997, 104), "At the meal they realize that not only has He accompanied them, but that they have drawn closer to Him. They have arrived. The closeness to Him has reached a point to where they are one with Him. The meal turns into the 'Feast of the Nearness to God'. God's relationship toward human beings becomes evident in this feast." Jesus, as he broke the bread, was telling his companions that he lives, that he has conquered death, and that he is and will be with them.

Once the accompanying stranger revealed himself, the process of transformation that began at the start of the trip intensified and moved them from desperation to hope, and from sadness to celebration. The self-discovery and knowledge of God was such that they felt completely liberated and happy to see again with the eyes of faith and hope: "Then their eyes were opened and they recognized him, and he disappeared from their sight" (Luke 24:31, NIV).

Once we see the light, we cannot hide it under a pillow. On the contrary, we place it in a conspicuous place so that other members of the community may also see. Once we meet the Lord, we will never again be the same. Once liberated from the blindness and oppression of sin, we have no alternative but to return to the community and share the experience that we have had with God: "We cannot help speaking about what we have seen and heard" (Acts 4:20, NIV).

In the reign of God, we do not hoard but rather share, be it our sorrows, our successes, or our happiness. "They got up and returned at once to Jerusalem. There they found the Eleven and those with them, assembled together" (Luke 24:33, NIV). These two travelers met God again, met themselves again, and met with their past. They were then ready to begin their lives and relate the story. They returned to their community to continue with their healing and journey toward wholeness.

4

THE COMMUNITY AS HEALING AGENT

I am the vine, you are the branches. Whoever remains in me and I in
him will bear much fruit, because without me you can do nothing.
—John 15:5 NIV

It seems a little bit irreverent to use this sacred text of our Christian tradition to convey the idea of community, but from our
Latino experience, these words uncover our intrinsic communitarian nature. Thus, if we were to continue with our irreverence,
we could reframe this passage from the Gospel of John to say that
it is in community that we bear much fruit, and by the same token,
outside of it we do nothing. But it is perhaps in this bold reading
of Jesus' own words where we can look beyond our individualistic
culture and glance at our collective forgotten self. For it was precisely in that collective spirit that we were created (Genesis 1:26),
and in that collective spirit where we hope to grow. "I pray also
for those who will believe in me through their message, that all of
them may be one, Father, just as you are in me and I am in you"
(John 17:20-21, NIV).

This is certainly not a nouveau interpretation of scriptures. As
Gustavo Gutiérrez (1994) cleverly formulates, the idea of encountering God among the community is as old as the history of the
Hebrew people. God promised to dwell among his people (Exodus
29:45-46), making his sanctuary among them (Ezekiel 37:27-28).
This promise takes a literal meaning in Christian tradition when
"the Word became flesh and made his dwelling among us" (John
1:14, NIV). Jesus himself addresses this communitarian nature of
God's dwelling when he establishes as a paradigm for judgment the
need to recognize his own presence in the least of our brothers and
sisters (Matthew 25:40). Finally, we notice how this idea continues
strong within the early Christian community by Paul's declaration
of our bodies as the temple of the Spirit (1 Corinthians 3:16-17). In
other words, we are the dwelling of God, and "remaining in God"
would also mean remaining in communion with each other.

Jürgen Moltmann (2000) reminds us that this communion reaches beyond the mere simplistic act of recognizing each other as living images of God. It also entails the promotion of the well-being of each member of the community. This action-oriented sense of communion is well exemplified in the passage of Acts 4:32-37, where it is said that the life of the Christian community is marked by the sharing of possessions and the absence of needy persons within the same.

Loughlan Sofield, Rosine Hammett, and Carroll Juliano (1998) write that it was because of the exemplification of this communal form of living that the early Christian community became a visible sign of God's abiding presence. The root of this connection is well established in New Testament theology in the writings of Paul, who in his letter to the Romans uses the analogy of the human body to teach us about the complementary nature of each one of the members of the community (1 Corinthians 12).

There is a witty fable that accurately depicts this same interconnection of the members of the community. This fable speaks of an intensely concerned mouse that runs in quest of help from other animals on the farm after having learned that the lady of the house has bought a new, powerful mousetrap that threatens the mouse's survival. The little mouse first turns to the hen in desperation, only to have the hen scorn his clamor, saying that it is not her problem if there is a new mousetrap on the farm. Then the mouse reaches out to the pig, running into a similar fate when the pig tells him that he is certainly concerned for his situation but does not want to have anything to do with it. Finally, the mouse consults with the farm's cow, which by the way is a very well-intentioned Christian. The cow exhorts the little mouse not to be concerned about such a situation because God will be there for him, and she sends the mouse away with the assurance of her prayers. Well, it happens that the same night, there is a horrific sound that cannot be confused with anything else but the new mousetrap clicking off. Listening to the thunderous sound, the lady of the house gets up to find out that the victim in the trap is not the mouse but a highly venomous serpent. Without much time to react, the lady is bitten by the serpent and taken to the hospital.

To encourage the healing of his wife, the owner of the farm kills the hen so he can make a nutritious soup for her. After several days, the lady is dismissed from the hospital with a poor prognosis. During her convalescence, many people come regularly to care for her at the farm. To provide food for all these people, the owner of the farm decides to kill the pig. Finally, the lady dies, and the cow is sacrificed so they can have enough food at the farm to feed all the people attending the wake and the funeral.

Even though we may be tempted to think that the misfortunes of others do not affect us, we are always touched by them in some way or another. We find a dramatic example of this in the terrible aftermath of Hurricane Katrina in New Orleans. We could accurately say each one of us living in America has been affected, as well as those who live beyond our own borders. But by the same token, the triumphs and successes of those within the community become our own triumphs and successes. In 2005, we saw an example of this after Lance Armstrong, who is a cancer survivor, won his seventh consecutive Tour de France. We could say that this was a triumph that somehow reached to all of us who at some point in our lives have experienced struggles and difficulties but have prevailed nonetheless.

This idea has predominated in our Latino/a communities, where historically we have been constantly threatened by stressors that are beyond our individual capacities. We have learned that it is by relying on each other that we are able to overcome the obstacles that form part of our daily living. This community is then the source of strength and the depository of resources that assist the individual in his or her quest to improve the given conditions of living.

It is important to notice that it is not our purpose to add more tension to the already-strained debate between individual and community. On the contrary, we believe these are complementary notions that work in harmony to serve the same purpose of restoring the image of God in us. By celebrating the individual uniqueness of each member of the community, we nourish the variety of gifts that identify the Christian community as the body of Christ. The idea is to value the uniqueness of each member of the community while keeping in mind the social responsibility of working together for the common good (Montilla 2004). The pastoral counselor who is community oriented is, in this sense, an agent who encourages the use of the community as a healing agent, since he or she has discovered that real help is found in this interaction between the individual and his or her surroundings (Lewis and Lewis 1983).

EMPOWERMENT AS A COMMUNITARIAN HEALING TOOL

Let us consider the case of José Ramirez, a thirty-seven-year-old Latino who immigrated to the United States in the early nineties after the economic recession in Mexico threatened to shatter the successful retail business that he had taken almost a decade to build. He came to live in southern Texas with his wife and their three children. Thanks to his experience, knowledge, and sagacity, José was able to regain economic independence in less than three years by buying and selling used cars. His family has adapted with ease to the customs of this part of the country, which on the surface do not differ in great measure from those back home. His children have already learned English and are doing very well in school.

Maria, his wife, has discovered that she is pretty well adapted to the independent lifestyle that she has been forced to live in the States. She is assisting at an ESL (English as a Second Language) school and has cultivated good friendships with some of her classmates, women who are going through similar circumstances. Because of his economic success, José has been able to pay a good lawyer to assist them with immigration affairs. In spite of all these favorable circumstances, José came looking for help for what he considers "a void in his life." After the first two interviews, his pastoral counselor begins to suspect that José's situation is being prompted by the lack of involvement in community affairs that were a vital part of his life in Mexico.

With this information in mind and ascertaining the community-relatedness of Latino/as, the pastoral counselor devises a plan of action that targets this social need of José's. Knowing that José is an enthusiast of soccer, the counselor suggests he join the weekly scramble that is sponsored by the Methodist church in town. Also beneficial might be to encourage José to become part of a local effort of Christian couples who weekly cross the border and serve primary needs of destitute families in and around Mexico's border with the United States. He can also follow the example of his wife and take advantage of educational opportunities that can serve him with a peer network while improving his innate abilities and skills. The pastoral counselor offers empowerment to José by enhancing his community experience while at the same time promoting social transformation and commitment.

In this example, several aspects of the pastoral counselor's role are important. All the information gathered during the pastoral assessment is helpful in presenting to José a point of reference that can offer viable options for addressing his concerns (Hershenson, Power, and Waldo 1996). This task of both gathering the information and presenting the point of reference is fundamental for the pastoral counselor working with Latino/as, inasmuch as environmental stressors are the primary source of conflict, especially for those who have only recently emigrated from other countries.

Herbert Goldenberg and Irene Goldenberg (2002) list some of the environmental stressors that the pastoral counselor needs to be alert to while working with Hispanics. Among these stressors are the generational level, the acculturation level, the languages spoken, the educational background, the socioeconomic status, rural or urban residence, adherence to cultural values, and religiosity or spirituality. We could also add to this list the immigration status, family-related stressors (distance from family, separation from loved ones, etc.), professional stressors (change of job function, new profession, etc.), and recreational stressors (hobbies, social network, etc.).

The second element we can identify as helpful in the work by the pastoral counselor in this specific case is the "strengths perspective" (Rappaport 1990). Judith A. Lewis and Michael D. Lewis (1983) remind us that if the community-oriented counselor is willing to see that which is harmful within the environmental surroundings of the individual, he or she might also be willing to utilize that which has the promise of health for the individual. In this case, there are several stressors that the pastoral counselor could have dwelt on as part of formulating José's problem—for instance, the short period of time that he and his family have been in the United States, the probable struggle with the language, and the loss of social connections. Instead, the pastoral counselor focused on environmental factors that could become a source of strength for José. Not only this, he or she recognized what José had to offer to make his community participation meaningful and oriented toward the common good, especially the common good of those less favored.

This meaningful community participation is precisely the process by which the individual is empowered as a fundamental instrument of community transformation. Empowerment, thus understood, is the use of individual skills and capacities (José's ability to dispose of free time, economic resources to attend to the needy, and the spiritual quest to enter into a meaningful encounter with God and others). Through community participation, the sense of control over one's own life can increase and effect positive change in others and self (Nelson, Lord, and Ochocka 2001). In other words, the idea of empowerment is not simply to help somebody become part of a given community, but to become an active agent of the same.

According to Geoffrey Nelson, John Lord, and Joanna Ochocka (2001, 173), "For us community support and integration means being a valued part of the community, not just being in community." By suggesting that José become part of the local effort of Christian couples serving the needs of poor Mexican families across the border, the pastoral counselor has offered José a great opportunity to utilize his gifts, abilities, and blessings in favor of the least of the kingdom. This is a good example of the shape that healing in community can take at any given time.

Nelson, Lord, and Ochocka (2001) identify a good number of positive outcomes that are among the advantages of promoting personal empowerment of individuals linked to the living being of their communities. Self-determination, decision making, perceptions of control, voice, skills, assertiveness, self-understanding, and self-esteem are all part of this process, which is initiated by inviting the individual to participate actively in the social development of those close to him or her.

We believe that by having been created in the image and likeness of God, we inherit from the Lord his most fundamental abilities, which are voice, power, and relatedness. We are then in the image of God when we are people with *voice*, people who are able to speak up and claim ownership of the blessings that are proper for our status of being almost like God (Psalm 8:5). Likewise, being in the image of God, we have *power* to change the unfair circumstances that deny us the possibilities of living in that image of God. Finally, *relatedness* means we do this in community; not by ourselves. We do this in union with others and God since we are essentially communal beings: "Then God said: 'Let us make humans in our image, after our likeness'" (Genesis 1:26 NIV). Empowerment then restores in us that image of God, which at times tends to get blurry and fuzzy, and restores that same image in those stripped of it by the unjust circumstances of our systems.

Finally, we can add assertiveness to the list of the counselor— in this case, the consideration that he or she gave to the "outsiders" within the community. Rappaport (1990, 52) suggests that the process of empowerment needs "to be committed to identifying, facilitating, or creating contexts, in which therefore silent and isolated people, those who are 'outsiders' in various settings . . . , gain understanding, voice, and influence over decisions that affect their lives." The pastoral counselor needs to be willing to offer social and personal empowerment even more to those outcast and marginalized, those who are neglected by the system, because they were precisely the ones whom Jesus, rephrasing the words of the prophet Isaiah, came to serve (Luke 4:18-19).

ECOLOGICAL COMMUNITY

One last consideration needs to be given to the ecological interconnection that is part of our communitarian nature. The term *ecology* is commonly used to designate our interactions with our surroundings (Hershenson et al. 1996; Lewis and Lewis 1983). These surroundings are either sociocultural, with other human beings and their body of beliefs and traditions, or physical, with our space surroundings and nature. In this sense, community does not simply refer to people; it also refers to animals, plants, and the earth and its elements.

It is meaningful that in the second narrative of creation (Genesis 2:4b-25) when God looked for a suitable partner for man, He first created animals (v. 19). Even though later in the text God finds a more suitable partner for man, the suitable character of animals is not completely lost. They remain a significant part of the development of our capacity to relate. By the act of naming the animals, humankind grows in the reclaiming of the likeness of God that allows us to care, respect, and love the Other. This act initiates for us a process of relatedness, a process that will evolve later on to allow our interactions with the neighbor, the community, and God.

The apprehension of the Latino experience through this eco-logical lens is then extremely important for the pastoral counselor seeking to promote growth. If we consider that at the root of our collective nature is our capacity to relate with our surroundings, we then need to consider that the practice of an ecological con-science is then a practice of connection. We connect with the beauty and mystical experience of creation. We connect with the self and its creative nature. Most importantly, we connect with others and God. Holistic growth and healing is thus fostered by promoting the respect and admiration that our Latino forebearers, our Mayans and Aztecs, felt for the crown of creation, earth, and its wild inhabitants.

5

A LATINO/A VIEW
OF SUFFERING AND ILLNESS

May its morning stars become dark;
may it wait for daylight in vain
and not see the first rays of dawn,
for it did not shut the doors of the womb on me
to hide trouble from my eyes.
"Why did I not perish at birth,
and die as I came from the womb?
Why were there knees to receive me
and breasts that I might be nursed?"
—Job 3:9-12 NIV

The joy of life for me would be to get up from this bed and be able to sit in my wheelchair, to look at people, to feel the breeze and the warmth of the sun. Being able to look up the sky and make figures out of the clouds, as I used to do with my little one. We would go out and looking at the clouds, where we would see alligators, horses, angels, and other figures, and we would play until she would get tired. Sometimes she would invite me to help her count sheep, and these sheep would be the little clouds that we would see roaming the sky. We would also climb onto the roof of our house and use a telescope to look at the stars and the moon during the night; it was a lot of fun. The joy of life for me would be to smell the fresh-cut grass and see the animals, all the little things.

These words belong to Gloria, a Latina patient forty-seven years of age, who spent several months in a local hospital. Gloria was a healthy and active woman with a successful career in the medical field. She worked hard for more than twenty years, helping patients in different hospitals of southern Texas, a predominantly Latino/a area. Because of an unfortunate event, Gloria has been rendered unable to breathe on her own for the past fourteen months, a condition that keeps her attached to ventilator support.

She has also lost most of her mobility and strength, and for the past six months has stayed mostly in bed. Due to the different complications not uncommon to patients under these conditions, Gloria has become a frequent visitor at our facility.

Gloria is deeply acquainted with pain and suffering. She not only attended to uncountable numbers of Latino/as at their most critical times, but she has also suffered in her own flesh the pains and restraints brought by illness. Her words speak of her resilience and profound sense of hope, which lead her to center her decimated energy on interactions with her daughter, other people, and nature. She prefers to visualize herself experiencing good times with her family rather than thinking of her suffering and agonizing treatment.

This episode clearly depicts for us the different dimensions that suffering can take at any given moment. Along this line of thought, Ronald B. Miller (2004) identifies three dimensions of suffering: physical, psychological, and social. These three dimensions are observable in Gloria, but the social nature of her suffering is what brings us closer to the heart of her anguish. "To look at people" was her first and foremost desire and the one that affected us the most in counseling. The rest of her dialogue continued under the same theme of "connection"—emotional and social connection with the people she loved and with creation. Community is at the heart of our Latino/a experience, and being separated from the social interactions characteristic of our upbringing could constitute the most excruciating and painful event in the lives of most Latino/a people.

It is an undeniable fact that the experience of suffering, as well as the experience of illness, is always culturally shaped (Kleinman 1988). The values and beliefs highly regarded by a culture are always at the core of the experience of the suffering person. For instance, in a Euro-American cultural frame, where individuality and independence are highly regarded, the elements feared in Gloria's situation would probably be her physical suffering and the dependence brought by her condition. Yet as we said of Gloria, her cultural experience, with family, community, and interdependence at the center, makes the single most powerful cause of her suffering the deprivation of such interactions.

This social nature of suffering is also observable in medical decision-making processes. There, the Latino/a patient regards as a duty the idea of preserving family members from the pain and the anxiety of these decisions (Kohlhasen 1995). In this sense, the suffering of the Latino/a patient assumes a redeeming value not strange to Latino/as predominantly Christian beliefs. As noted by Miller (2004), suffering in relation to Christianity is usually associated with martyrdom or the idea of expiatory suffering, where suffering has a meaning and a purpose. This element of bravado and sacrifice in the midst of suffering is well regarded and appreciated in Latino/a circles, especially for women, who are commonly encouraged to suffer patiently, following the example of the Virgin Mary (Jesus' mother in Christian tradition), a phenomenon known as "marianismo" (Cauce and Domenech-Rodriguez 2002). This vicarious suffering could be seen in Gloria's assertion of preferring to suffer than to see one of her relatives go through that painful experience: "I am glad it happened to me and not to anybody else in my family." This attitude toward suffering is also encouraged in Latino men, but mostly as an individualistic display of strength rather than as a redemptive social sacrifice.

Eric J. Cassell (1992) adds another dimension of suffering that we consider fundamentally important for the pastoral counselor: the spiritual dimension. This is certainly not an easy topic to summarize, considering the numerous variations that this suffering is likely to take. Latino/a people might experience spiritual suffering when facing the dilemma of voicing their frustration and anger for what they could consider an unjust suffering while reconciling this protest with the idea of a compassionate and loving God. Spiritual suffering could also be observed in the faithful believer who fears coming to grips with his or her illness and, further, cannot trust his or her almighty and suffering God, a God able to heal and give life to the dead. Not uncommon is the suffering patient who is tormented by guilt because of what he or she believes is a punishment from God. These are only a few examples, but in them we can appreciate the weight of the spiritual dimension of suffering, a dimension that, because of our strong religious heritage, becomes a decisive component of ministering and counseling within the Latino/a community.

SUFFERING MEETS ILLNESS

Besides being culturally shaped, illness usually takes on an individual character, making use of the person's experiences. As written by Arthur Kleinman (1988, 5), "We can also say of illness experience that it is always distinctive." Nonetheless, some characteristics are particular to the Latino/a view of illness and somehow reflect the same element of interconnection that includes nature, community, and even supernatural powers as part of the illness event. Thus, in Latino/a communities, it is not uncommon to encounter an open discussion and acknowledgment of sickness as a curse that has the power to strengthen the illness and even to cause death (Kolhasen 1995). Of course, not every Latino/a person believes that if you speak out and admit you're sick, that your health condition will worsen. However, it is a reality that remains present in our day and age, especially within some Evangelical communities. Similarly, other elements of the Latino culture are shared by some and rejected by others, but continue to exert some influence in the Latino/a view of suffering and illness.

One of these elements is *curanderismo*, which is rather popular and widely spread among the diverse faces of our Latino/a identity. *Curanderismo* is a mixture of Spanish, African, and indigenous beliefs and ideas that places illness within three categories: environmental imbalance, malevolent force, and psychological factors (Kohlhasen 1995). It is in the power and insight of the *curandero* (faith healer) to treat the ill person by considering all three of these categories. Environmental imbalance refers to fields of energy, either positive or negative, that might be affecting the ill person. Malevolent forces are associated with a particular source, usually another person who either wants to hurt or gain the favor (love) of somebody else. Psychological factors are commonly treated with beverages, and they respond to what Euro-American medicine would call stress. Nowadays, this idea of *curanderismo* is taking on new facades that are normally concealed under scientific (astrological) terms but that in reality represent the same.

Another of the elements that could be encountered as part of the composed Latino/a view on illness is fatalism or determinism (Kohlhasen 1995), which we mentioned in the discussion of the spiritual dimension of suffering. Under this notion, the person believes that everything is predestined and that his or her suffering needs to be accepted without reproach as the will of God. In this case, accepting the will of God is actually a healthy element that needs to be considered while counseling with ill patients. The problem resides in the refusal to voice resentment, anger, frustration, and like feelings that are commonly associated with the experience of illness. Such a refusal ends up becoming a stumbling block in our effort to help the person process his or her unfavorable condition. In this sense, the pastoral counselor as a reminder of God's presence has the authority and the responsibility of empowering the person to voice the anguish that such an event is causing in his or her life.

Finally, C.W. Kohlhasen (1995) mentions "Latino holism" as the idea that tends to attribute supernatural causes to the experience of illness. He describes three principles or levels of causality related to illness: immediate causes (pathogens, malignancies), underlying causes (exposure to infection), and ultimate causes (stress, poor diet, lack of exercise). As observed by Kohlhasen, this ultimate level of causality of illness is the one most often utilized by Latino/as. This reasoning anoints the task of the pastoral counselor with greater authority while counseling with Latino/a patients/consultees. Thus, the pastoral counselor also becomes an agent of strength, support, and even healing (emotional, spiritual, and sometimes physical) for the Latino/a patient who has linked his or her illness with its ultimate causes.

THE ORIGIN OF EVIL

The problem of suffering and illness is closely related to the theological discussion on the origin of evil. Considering the strong influence that Christianity has had over our Latino/a idiosyncrasy, it is not strange to find that our understanding of the origin of evil is mostly dependent on the biblical explanation and interpretation of the same. Within this context, we find two basic theoretical approaches. Using William James's (1902/2004) terminology, we could call them the "melancholic" or "morbid-minded" approach and the "healthy-minded" approach. The melancholic approach sees evil as an essential part of our human nature, and the healthy-minded approach sees evil as good or as good in the making. Even though the dominant interpretation of the origin of evil in Christian tradition is markedly melancholic, both of these approaches have components that are important to consider when helping our Latino/a communities.

Under the Christian tradition's dominant interpretation of the origin of evil, humankind was created to be free from suffering and death. It was only because of the transgression of Adam and Eve (our forebearers) that we are condemned to experience the pangs of birth and to labor for our bread (Genesis 3:16, 19). Death also is a by-product of this first transgression or act of disobedience (Romans 5:12; 1 Corinthians 15:21-22) and, as such, something foreign to our true nature. Thus, suffering and illness are a corruption of that original purpose of God's creation, and we men and women hold the primary responsibility for such a condition because of our sinful act in Paradise.

This interpretation was initially woven by Augustine, and since then it has permeated most of the Christian and even non-Christian world. Augustine talks about a "fallen nature" that can be redeemed only by grace, and as part of that fallen nature, we are predisposed to illness and all sorts of difficulties. Even medical aid is a punishment in itself as seen by Augustine: "The cures and remedies are themselves tortures, so that men are delivered from a pain that destroys by a cure that pains" (Paolucci 1962/1996, 5). This quote is taken from Augustine's best-known work, *The City of God*. In this work, Augustine contrasts the kingdom of God with our human kingdoms (republics), which are a mere unfair representation of the former. In this sense, Augustine's discourse greatly resembles the philosophy of Plato (Tannenbaum and Schultz 1998), who made a similar comparison with the myth of the cave in *The Republic*, his most famous work.

This association of ideas between Plato and Augustine gives origin to what Dorothee Soelle (1975) has called "Christian Masochism." This term explains the repudiation of the human body as a channel of vice and sin, and the acceptance of physical suffering as a form of building temperance and deepening the deprecation of our bodies. This idea is born out of the Christianized philosophy of Plato, which contrasts body and soul as two different components of the human person. This idea was carried on in Augustine's theology and has been part of the religious understanding of our Latino/a communities. The soul becomes the divine light that abides in us and allows us to have a glimpse of what is waiting for us in our heavenly kingdom. In contrast, our bodies represent the irrefutable proof of our fallen nature; they are corruptible and susceptible to vice and illness.

Roger E. Olson (2002) mentions the tendency to use a triple division of the human person into body, soul, and spirit. In this sense, the soul is associated with the person's consciousness and as such is not immortal. For those who believe in this "trichotomy," the spirit is the immortal part of the person, the part that is able to enter into communion with the divine. Nonetheless, the idea of fragmenting the human person remains at the core of this interpretation. Moreover, the difference between terms such as *soul* and *spirit* has proved to be confusing and commonly misunderstood. It can then be expected that, at least outside academic discussions, we will hear these terms used in counseling Latino/as indistinctly to address that which is considered immortal and incorruptible in us.

This dichotomy (or trichotomy) of the body as understood by most of the Christian world represents a serious threat that undermines the principle of integrity of the human being so well regarded by the Hebrew and early Christian traditions (Olson 2002). Even though our bodies were created out of the "dust of the earth" (Genesis 2:7), God proclaimed them as being "very good" (Genesis 1:31). Thus, we will doubt God's wisdom when we insist in calling bad something that God declares good. As pastoral counselors, we see much value in the concept of "person" or "personhood" as a liberating concept that allows us to strive toward a wholesome outlook on our humanity. The term *person* highlights our value as the pinnacle of God's creation and reminds us of our need to care for and love ourselves as children of God.

This is the spirit of the writings of Irenaeus (130–202 CE), whom we could consider the father of the healthy-minded approach to the origin of evil. Interpreting the biblical passage of Genesis 1:26, Irenaeus speaks of the "image" and "likeness" of God as two essentially different notions. According to Irenaeus, we are created as the "image" of God, and although we are affected by sin, this image is not completely lost or damned, because it hopes for finally achieving the "likeness" of God. This road to the likeness of God is paved by our free responses to evil and suffering and the ways we dare to participate in promoting good out of this same evil. Thus, evil serves a purpose, which Hans Urs Von Balthasar (1988, 231) later interpreted as an "educational means."

The difference between these two approaches is immeasurably great and the implications that both bring to the interpretation of suffering and illness are out of proportion to the interpretation. John H. Hick (1990, 45) clearly portrays this experience: "Whereas the Augustinian theology sees our perfection as lying in the distant past, in an original state long since forfeited by the primordial calamity of the fall, the Irenaean type of theology sees our perfection as lying before us in the future, at the end of a lengthy and arduous process of further creation through time."

Irenaeus's interpretation and approach to the problem of evil, although mainly speculative (Olson 2002), offers a different perspective that has been neglected within our long Christian history. The prevalence of the melancholic approach has embodied many evils of its own and has left our communities yearning for a different message that dwells on what is good in them, because our faults do not cease being obvious. It does not mean that the healthy-minded approach is perfectly appropriate and without blemish. Besides the aforementioned lack of biblical foundation in this message, we recognize with James (1902/2004) that this approach carries the danger of denying the reality of suffering. Suffering and evil are real. They are constantly challenging our understanding and our faith, and letting them masquerade behind soft-sounding words is but a mere distraction. However, the choice between dwelling on this suffering or accepting it as a natural part of our lives, and even cherishing it, is a totally different thing.

As Soelle (1975) remarks, the Augustinian attitude only serves the purpose of lowering our self-esteem, and good self-esteem is not precisely the greatest virtue of our Latino/a communities. We have enough oppressors in the media, the economic and political system, and the long history of racism and discrimination to make of our faith one more oppressor. Our faith, as proclaimed by Jesus, is about bringing freedom to the oppressed and the captive, sight to the blind, good news to the poor (Luke 4:18-19). In summary, our faith is about restoring those who have been historically marginalized, which means restoring the image of our Latino/a people, restoring the value of their struggles and suffering, and restoring what is good and has been proclaimed good in them.

In Gloria's case, we can effect this restoration by acknowledging her suffering, a suffering that is real and can take different forms (physical, psychological, social, and spiritual). We provide Gloria with the opportunity to relate, share, and communicate her experience, while as pastoral counselors we can validate and offer a point of reference in which she can see her suffering face-to-face. It is quite common to hear relatives, friends, and even clergy encouraging, sometimes demanding that the patient surrender to the illness and the suffering, while at the same time they negate and suppress the opportunity that the patient needs to make sense of his or her suffering in his or her own terms. While spending time with Gloria, we would hear comments such as, "You don't need to be depressed," "You're doing well; you don't need to be sad," and, "You need to get in a better mood so you can go home." All these comments and many similar others were said with good intention but served only as a momentary fix. The suffering person may force a smile or simply acknowledge the advice, but the truth is that comments like these only fragment the self even more, adding destructive feelings of guilt to the already distressed individual. With these comments, Gloria may feel that it is partly her fault that she is under this condition, but she finds little that she can do to remedy her episodes of depression and sadness. Confused by the message, Gloria probably would find it more difficult to come to terms with her suffering. The pastoral counselor remedies this by sojourning with the suffering person and recognizing that as caregivers we are also subject to similar struggles.

COUNSELING IN THE MIDST OF SUFFERING

We began this chapter by quoting from the book of Job, which in Hebrew and Christian tradition has been considered to describe the epitome of suffering. Job was a faithful servant of God (1:8) who was subject to a myriad of calamities, including the loss of his economic resources, children, and even his health. In the midst of this ominous series of events, he receives a visit from three of his friends (2:11), Eliphaz, Bildad, and Zophar. Seeing Job in his suffering, these three friends act as effective and competent pastoral counselors by sitting with Job in silence for seven days and seven nights (2:13). This helpful presence changes when Job breaks the silence and speaks (3:1), uttering his frustration and rage at what has been happening to him: "Why did I not perish at birth?" (3:11). By doing this, he incites the theological responses of his friends, who insist on finding guilt in Job or his family, because they do not see how an innocent man could be suffering as Job is suffering (8:3-4; 11:6; 15:5; 20:1-29). During the whole discourse, Job continues justifying himself and trying to voice his anger; he even asks his friends (counselors) to be quiet and listen (13:6, 13; 16:4-6). The story is only interrupted in Job 32, when a new character, Elihu, appears. The scripture says Elihu was a young man who seemingly listened to Job and his friends and was enraged with Job and his justification (32:2). Finally, God answers Job and speaks of his great power and justice, and then addresses Job's friends. He tells them how angry he is because they spoke what is not true about God (42:7). Job intercedes for his friends in prayer, and then all his prosperity returns. As an interesting point, part of the final restoration of God to Job includes the participation of the community (relatives and friends), who came to visit Job and "consoled him and comforted him for all the adversities that the LORD had brought on him" (42:11 NASB).

In his classic work on the psychology of suffering, David Bakan (1968, 4) writes, "Pain produces the outcry which evokes help by others." In the book of Job, this is the first dynamic we observe. Distressed by Job's pain, his friends rush to help him. It is a natural response, and almost everyone does it out of goodwill, but as we have noticed before, goodwill is not enough. The pastoral counselor needs to be prepared and trained to minister in times of suffering; otherwise he or she would probably do more damage than good. Particularly important in this situation is the heightened anxiety that the counselor seems to experience. The untrained pastoral counselor, unaware of what is happening, would rush into action, which is really treating the counselor's own anxiety. An example of this would be a pastoral counselor who, after facing Gloria's suffering, would promptly elaborate theological discourses or explanations: "You are sharing in God's suffering; offer it up to God." Or the pastoral counselor, facing Gloria's suffering, might rush into prayer. Finally, the pastoral counselor, looking to curtail his or her anxiety, might become a hospitality worker, content to pass out water or coffee to family members. Overcoming the initial anxiety that pain and suffering bring us requires a conscious effort that does not shun our feelings but recognizes them while being able to place them apart and thereby attend to the needs of the suffering person.

Job's friends are very good at understanding that the best thing they have to offer is their presence, and they do so by sitting in silence with Job for seven entire days. Silence is a dreadful thing, especially when it is accompanied by moans of pain and outcries of suffering. Many times Gloria could not even utter a word. She would just lie in bed and look at people. Who knows what was going through her mind? Sitting a few minutes with her and trying to share in her forced silence was very difficult. In the story of Job, he was the first one to break the silence, signifying the completeness of his friends' presence. They were fully present, and they would have done a beautiful job if they had just remained silent. The pastoral counselor values silence as the best ally in his or her effort to communicate God's compassion and love to those in suffering and illness.

But Job's friends were not only present; they also recognized the language of suffering and were able to communicate in that language. In the first chapter of the book of Job, the scripture tells us that Job tears his cloak, cuts his hair, and prostrates himself to the ground, expressing his suffering (1:20-22). Then when Job's friends arrive, the scripture narrates almost verbatim the same actions done by them: "They began to weep aloud; they tore their cloaks and threw dust upon their heads" (2:12 NIV), adding that they sat on the ground. It is important for us as pastoral counselors to recognize that the language of suffering is broader than what we usually conceive. Groans, laments, tears, screams, and like behaviors considered inappropriate in most of our interactions are quite understandable in moments of suffering, and the counselor needs to be prepared for them. Miller (2004, 44) perfectly expresses this language of suffering when he writes, "Yet human suffering involves the unspeakable, unbearable, horrible experience of life. It often defies verbal expression and can be expressed only through facial expressions, cries and groans, contortions of the body and face, or a breakdown in bodily functions."

Since the pastoral counselor represents an anchor for the distraught and disorganized person in suffering, it is not advisable for him or her to engage in this kind of behavior (groans, moans, screams, laments, and so on). However, we have witnessed occasions in which the tears of a moved pastoral counselor became the most powerful intervention the counselor could offer. Nonetheless, it remains a risky scenario that is best to keep under check. In this sense, the value of what Eliphaz, Bildad, and Zophar did was to use the language of the consultee, meaning use of a tone, speed, and rate of language is similar to that being used by the person in need of our help and support. This is a difficult task to accomplish with Gloria, since her speech is dramatically affected by her tracheotomy. In this case, we relied heavily on body language, such as sitting down, leaning toward her, breathing deeply, and trying to reflect, almost mirror, her demeanor.

Our three biblical counselors did excellent work until, incited by Job's words, they decided to break their silence. From that point on, they did everything a counselor is *not* supposed to do. They preached at Job, they denied Job the opportunity to voice his discomfort and anger, they repeatedly acted as God's protectors ("do not say that of God," "God is not like that," and so on), and they refused to consider Job's position and simply stopped listening to him. As Gustavo Gutiérrez (1985) points out, these friends with their elaborate theological speeches did nothing but produce foolish words and almost blasphemous responses to the situation. Even after Job explicitly asked them to listen to him (13:5-6), they remained unaware of his request. These counselors were so focused on bringing their point across that they totally forgot their initial goal of traveling together to give Job "sympathy and comfort" (3:11).

We emphasized Job's words in provoking his friends' reaction because (aside from this being what the scripture says in verse 4:1), it is a frequent occurrence among those offering pastoral counseling. People usually test our beliefs and confront our understanding in basic truths. Faith and God are two of the most susceptible themes that a pastoral counselor sees challenged time after time while confronting people during suffering. Only a pastoral counselor who, through training, has been able to test his or her beliefs would be able to confidently face any provocation without reacting or defending his or her posture. The task of the pastoral counselor is a very different one, since he or she does not stand in front of the person as an expert, but as a fellow pilgrim. As addressed by Miller (2004), the task of the counselor confronted by suffering is to hear, accept, and acknowledge the wrong done to the person. Miller talks about the authority that is invested in the counselor as a gatekeeper of health and normality, and in this role, he or she validates—or, using Miller's words, legitimizes—the suffering of the one anointing him or her with this authority.

After fourteen months of suffering, Gloria still finds it helpful to hear words that recognize the agony of her condition. From time to time, she needs to hear from those close to her that what she is going through is very difficult. She needs to hear that it is OK to feel that it is unfair to be deprived of those wonderful moments in the company of her daughter, her husband, and the people she wholeheartedly misses. Gloria needs to hear that it is hard to depend on others for almost everything. She needs to hear that she is braver than most of us, and that we owe her respect for the valiant manner with which she faces her pain and discomfort. Finally, she needs to hear that with her smile and radiance, she inspires others to face with courage the rough passages of our lives. She needs to hear that, although unjustified, her suffering could have meaning and that she has the right to protest and voice her frustration and anger. Job has usually been portrayed as an archetype of patience, but the truth is that he was far from being patient. Gutiérrez (1985) calls him a "rebellious believer," because as Gutiérrez points out, he rebels against the suffering of the innocent and the theological discourse that justifies it.

The pastoral counselor acts then as the instrument that helps the suffering person voice the physical, psychological, social, and spiritual pain that comes with his or her condition. The counselor becomes an amplifier of the discontent brought by illness and the nuances of hospitals, doctors, and medicines. In doing so, the counselor allows the person to own his or her suffering and confront it with conviction because, for once, the counselor has seen the face of suffering and can look it in the eyes without dread. The face of suffering is a human face that can be called by name. The face of Latino/a suffering is a human face that calls us by name: Gloria.

6

ETHICS FROM A LATINO/A PERSPECTIVE

Carla is a fifty-year-old Latina born in Mexico and living in the United States of America since she was twelve. She completed high school and earned a college degree in education in California. For the last twenty years, she has been living in Texas, where she has worked as a high school science teacher. Carla describes herself as a committed Evangelical Christian and serves in her church as a Sunday school teacher. She is married and has four grown children, three sons and one daughter. Her youngest son, Pedro, is twenty-four years old and has had some legal problems, mostly related to drug abuse. Three weeks ago the police came by her house, looking for her son after they had attempted to stop him for speeding. When the officer had stepped out of his patrol car, Pedro had fled the scene on his motorcycle and disappeared. The state's department of motor vehicles showed that the motorcycle license plate was issued to Pedro and that he was living at his mother's address. For that reason, the police came to her home looking for him. They asked Carla if Pedro was inside, and she responded that he had moved and had not contacted her in three months. She offered her business card and kindly asked the officer to please let her know if he hears about Pedro because she is worried about his whereabouts.

The truth was that Pedro was inside the house and hiding in his room. Carla was completely aware of that. How would Carla reconcile her Christian faith with her action? Were Carla's principles of veracity and loyalty to the family in tension? What principles and values informed Carla's decision-making process? What are Carla's views on justice and honesty?

Carla came for pastoral counseling not because she was worried about her decision or because she was feeling guilty about it, but rather she came because she wanted to explore options for her son's issues with drug abuse. Latino/a ethics has been highly influenced by females, who more often are the ones making decisions about finances, health, education, and relationships for their families. Thus, Latino ethics, as in many collective societies, has three key components: compassion, solidarity, and loyalty to community. Most decisions are made considering these three elements. Carla decided to be truthful to her motherhood duty, compassionate with her son, in solidarity with her family, and loyal to her community. She also recognized that Pedro needed help and decided to take action to assist him. Another factor that perhaps affected Carla's decision was that the police force is often seen by the Latino/a community as an instrument of the oppressor or, at the very least, part of the oppressive system.

JUSTICE

When people see ethics from the periphery, they reinterpret traditional understanding of principles and their order of priorities. For instance, the principle of justice merely refers to *suum cuique tribuere* (to give everybody his or her due, or to render to each his or her own) as presented from the people in power. This reading on distributive/proportionate justice has been used to masquerade injustice and inequality. Justice in the Hispanic context transcends distributive justice to include a justice with solidarity that takes sides with the oppressed and marginalized. For Latino/as, justice cannot be understood or applied separately from other principles such as equality, liberty, solidarity, compassion, loyalty, *respeto,* and community. Therefore, to say "social justice" is redundant; justice cannot be understood separate from one's relation with others.

EQUALITY

Human beings as created in the image of God have a voice, power, and capacity to live in intimacy with self, others, nature, and Creator. This image implies that all humans are equal but not identical. However, this image does not have a color (black, white, brown, yellow) or gender/sex (male or female). This image of God cannot be imaged but seen and experienced in connection with the diverse mosaics found in humankind. This equality calls for equal rights, access, and opportunities for everyone in all areas of activity. Again, as in justice, equality cannot be understood apart from a social-relational context.

We purposely separate equality from justice to emphasize that some equal treatment could be unjust. For instance, to apply the same psychological testing to Hispanics and whites could be unjust, as most of these tests have not been created or standardized with the Latino/a population in mind. In this sense, equality could be applicable only within the cultural context. Another example is that most entry exams for college and graduate school are applied equally to all people. Many Latino/as attend school where the technology, educational personnel, and financial resources are very limited. Therefore, to require an equal entry exam is unjust. In addition, these tests limit intelligence to logic and reasoning, where collectivist societies have a broader understanding of intelligence, which includes the ability to relate and live harmoniously with self, others, and nature. The same is true for access to credit, healthcare, and housing. Human beings are equal and deserve to be treated with respect, concern, dignity, and contextual justice.

LIBERTY/FREEDOM

The words *liberty* and *freedom* refer to the immeasurable capacities and potential of human beings to choose and design the destiny of their lives. This speaks to the capacity that was given since the beginning, when humans were created in the image of God, with the ability to choose between good and bad. In this we insert the thought from Irenaeus (c. 115–202 CE), who submits that the sin of Adam and Eve was to doubt their identity and power. Their response to the tempter should have been, "We are already like God" because we were created in God's image, so we already have the power to distinguish right and wrong. The people in power, religious and political alike, have invented "scientific" and "theological" foundations to show that human beings are incapable of deciding for themselves, so they need the church and the state to do it for them. This could be seen in Augustine's (354–430 CE) idea of original sin and its ramifications.

We purposely prefer to use *liberty* and *freedom* instead of the commonly known principle of autonomy, because the power to choose is contextual and the decision made takes into consideration the impact on self, others, nature, and Creator. The belief that human beings have the power, competence, and capacity to

organize and direct their lives in the best functional and satisfactory way is central to the principles of liberty and freedom. Even
in situations when persons, because of biological or psychological reasons, cannot decide for themselves, their caregivers and
loved ones should choose as if the decision were being made by
the handicapped persons. This is possible in a community where
members know each other and seek the best for the others. We are
free to serve God and others: "Let My people go, that they may
serve Me" (Exodus 8:1, NASB). We are free to be like God: just,
compassionate, humble, abounding in love, and seekers of peace
(Isaiah 9:6; Jonah 4:2; Hosea 2:19; Matthew 5:9).

Liberty and freedom imply that people trusting their God-
given talents and power direct and guide their own lives. The fact
that the community of faith is consulted and used in the process
of making a decision does not take away the person's responsibility for the course of his or her action. In this sense, the gods,
angels, demons, or others are not in control of people' lives. God
and the community have equipped us to make wise and educated
decisions, but we cannot blame them for the outcome. Healthy
communities encourage this type of locus of control, as it has been
shown that people do better in their studies, work, and relationships when this kind of liberty and freedom is promoted (Lefcourt
1982; Findley and Cooper 1983; Miller et al. 1986; Peterson and
Barrett 1987; Tangney et al. 2004).

SOLIDARITY

Throughout many years of oppression and subjugation, the key
survival tool of Latino/as has been solidarity. The idea of coming
alongside the sufferer and marginalized is applauded by most Hispanic communities. Jesus' parable of the good Samaritan, which
he used in response to the question "Who is my neighbor?" (Luke
10:29), is a good illustration of what solidarity is all about. The
story points out that the man in need was naked and unconscious,
making it impossible to tell this person's nationality or ethnicity.
He was a complete stranger.

A Samaritan sojourner was also coming from Jerusalem to
Jericho, and when he saw the man who was beaten and broken,
he was moved with such compassionate love that he assisted him

without considering his status or ethnicity. The Samaritan was himself a marginalized person who had experienced the pain of discrimination and racism. He understood what it meant to be oppressed and exploited. The Samaritan showed solidarity with this stranger and made this man's pain and struggle his issues. He was willing to take the risk and become vulnerable to help a fellow traveler. He was willing to sacrifice his comfort and personal commitments on behalf of a brother. Moved by compassion and empathy, he felt responsibility for the one who was hurting and decided to help. This Samaritan knew that the quality of his life was linked to the quality of this sufferer's life. He made this man happy, and by doing that, he experienced humanity to the fullest. This sense of mutuality guides most Latino/as' ethical process. Solidarity means that we are in this together and together we will do it. Who is my neighbor? The oppressed, the marginalized, the downtrodden, the stranger, our brothers and sisters who come from the west, east, south, and north.

Leonardo Boff (2001) says *solidaridad* starts with the premise that all that exists is interconnected, interdependent, and has a common origin and destiny. We have similar wounds, analogous struggles, and corresponding joys, and we embrace common hopes and utopias. Indeed, solidarity is our condition in life and in death. As Martin Luther King Jr. (1963) wrote from the Birmingham City Jail, "We are caught in an inescapable network of mutuality, tied in a single garment of destiny. Whatever affects one directly affects all indirectly."

COMPASSION

The Hebrew Bible portrays God as a compassionate and gracious God who abounds in love and faithfulness (Psalm 86:15). Compassion encompasses emotions and actions. We feel empathy and do whatever is possible to alleviate or eliminate the suffering of our brothers and sisters. The call from our Creator is to be as compassionate as he is (Luke 6:36). Compassion compels us to act as coworkers with God in the process of alleviating people's afflictions. Compassion implies a commitment to dispose oneself, to receive the other into one's "home-space," to weep and laugh together, to breathe the same air, to speak at the same tone, and to sit at the same level (Marcel 1950). The love for one another is what empowers us to welcome strangers into our own lives (1 Peter 4:8-9). An ethical decision will reflect this compassion and deep awareness of oneness.

LOYALTY AND FIDELITY

One of the most important elements of human relationships is loyalty or fidelity to the person, instead of to institutions. To betray one's family is unthinkable in most Hispanic communities. This could explain Carla's falsehood with the police officers. She understood that her first allegiance was to protect her son with all her heart, mind, body, and spirit. She did not have an ethical dilemma, as she knew that her son would have a better chance to get healed in a rehab center than at the county jail. Her love for him defined her loyalty and fidelity. Her sense of loyalty and love was such that she would be willing to go to jail instead of letting her son's hope for recovery vanish.

RESPETO

The principle of *respeto* to the person implies accepting people's diverse ideas, emotions, and relationships. *Respeto* invites us to recognize that our brothers and sisters are being created in the image of God and have incalculable value, nontransferable and permanent, that does not change because of sex, gender, ethnicity, religious preference, age, political affiliation, marital status, physical challenges, and lifestyles. *Respeto* compels us to avoid discriminating, to take responsibility for the impact of our decisions on ourselves, others, and nature, and to fight for the well-being of the other.

Respeto compels us to keep confidentiality and not use people's stories as illustrations for sermons. Respecting the person implies taking time to explain the scope and limitations of confidentiality. For instance, if the consultee's information is going to be shared with third-party payers, the consultee must be informed of such possibilities before the therapeutic relationship starts. Similarly, counselors should explain that if there is child abuse, it creates some legal ramifications that may obligate pastoral counselors to notify authorities.

"Am I my brother's keeper?" (Genesis 4:9). Yes, we are our brothers' and sisters' keepers. We respect each other, nature, and earth, and recognize that because of our interconnectedness, we are part of the same web of life, so we seek to act responsibly by mutually protecting and caring for each other.

A holistic ethic respects the complexity, diversity, and uniqueness of people and nature. A holistic ethic puts the earth, not the human, at the center. We are charged with caring for the planet (Genesis 2:15). This is the essence of ethics (*ethos* with eta, η, our dwelling place, our cosmic house): a commitment to create a safe atmosphere and an environment where life can be experienced to the fullest. To achieve that, we develop ethics (*ethos* with epsilon, ε), sketch out plans of action, implement rules, create norms, and follow customs that are conducive to the protection and enrichment of the "house." Within a holistic ethics, we do not take advantage of or exploit people for our own benefit or to meet particular personal needs. We understand that our happiness and survival hinge on the existence and contentment of others—people as well as nature.

7

EDUCATION AND LEARNING IN THE LATINO/A POPULATION

Juan is the American-born son of immigrants from Honduras. After graduating from high school two years ago, Juan decided to go to college with the hope of eventually becoming a lawyer. Juan was the first in the family to attend college, daring to defy his two older brothers, who disapproved of Juan's educational ideals. After his first semester in college, Juan finally gave in to the pressures from home and decided to leave school and join the family business. Juan now has a baby with his girlfriend, and although "from time to time" he thinks of school, he does not consider it a viable possibility.

Maria is a seventeen-year-old third-generation Latina with two daughters. Maria dropped out of school before finishing the eighth grade. She now lives with her common-law husband, who is the father of her second child. Maria does not consider school a possibility. She talks about "eventually" getting her GED (General Educational Development diploma), but "not now with the babies and all."

Carlos is a thirty-two-year-old Latino immigrant who has been living in Houston for almost eight years. He works in construction with a leveling crew, and his hourly wage is ten dollars. Carlos has been working in this job for the last four years. During those years, because of his lack of knowledge of the English language, he has lost numerous possibilities to become a supervisor and increase his hourly wage by at least five dollars. Carlos has tried diverse methods of learning English, but he quickly becomes discouraged and abandons his mission.

Juan, Maria, and Carlos are representative of the stories of many Latino/as in U.S. communities. Together, their stories tell of a sad reality that is perpetuating itself in our day. In spite of being responsible for the great increases in student enrollments (U.S. Department of Education [DOE] 2001), Latino/as continue to have the highest dropout rate from secondary school: 28 percent, compared with 7 percent among whites and 13 percent among Black Americans (DOE 2003). This means that more than a quarter of our Latino/a population will never finish secondary school. Likewise, 27 percent of the Latino/a population, like Maria, has less than a ninth-grade education, compared with 4 percent of whites (Ramírez and de la Cruz 2002). Furthermore, Latino/as have the highest birth rate between the ages of fifteen and nineteen, with statistics showing that these men and women are less likely to finish high school (DOE 2003).

This pattern does not change much with Latino/a students who actually graduate from high school and continue on to college. Although we lack precise information on Latino/a college dropout rates, estimates suggest that approximately 30 percent of Latino/a students abandon higher-education institutions in their first year (DOE 1998). Moreover, the National Center for Education Statistics (DOE 2003) estimates the college completion rate of Latino/as as a mere 10 percent for persons between twenty-five and twenty-nine years of age. This is compared with 34 and 18 percent completion rates among whites and Blacks, respectively. In the area of on-the-job training, there is not much difference. In the disadvantages faced by Latino/as, one bright spot is that this racial-ethnic group is most likely to take English as a Second Language classes (DOE 2003), instilling in us some hope for Carlos and his future as a supervisor with his leveling crew.

These basic statistics are simply the reflection of a reality that has been neglected in many ways. Our pastoral role is not outside of this responsibility. On the contrary, we need to remember that we have been summoned to use the gifts that help to build the church (1 Corinthians 14:12), and among them, the gift of teaching or instruction is given a privileged place (1 Corinthians 12:28). One cannot help but appreciate the wisdom of the Spirit in signaling teaching as a building tool, because it is by teaching that we are able to inform people, give them hope, and cocreate in the divine plan of God's kingdom.

Building the kingdom of God requires more than building (teaching). It requires revising and changing. It requires uprooting and pulling down. With the prophet Jeremiah, we are called to break the chains that have kept us slaves of an educational system that is perpetuating a history of oppression and neglect. Although Jeremiah was given authority to build and to plant, the conditions for this act of building were set by the act of destroying and overthrowing (Jeremiah 1:10). We, as pastoral counselors, have been given the same responsibility to recreate the conditions that would make the education of our Latino/a people a liberating act.

To carry on with this mission, we need to become familiar with the theories that have been at the root of our educational system. Within these surroundings, we will be able to look at the ideas that shape and define the way we teach our communities. In this environment, our teaching ministry turns into a prophetic mission that allows us to denounce the failing practices of an educational system that has not yet reached the needs of our Latino/a communities.

LEARNING THEORIES

From behaviorism to cognitive-constructivism

A considerable number of learning theories have resulted from a marked interest in the field during a great part of the twentieth century (Bigge and Shermis 2004). Although they are numerous, we could easily distribute these theories between two ends, having at one end the behaviorist approach and at the other end the cognitive-constructivist approach. Some others, including Morris L. Bigge and Samuel S. Shermis, prefer to call the latter the "cognitive interactionist" theories, because this perspective emphasizes environmental interaction. We nonetheless prefer the *constructivist* term emphasized by Dale H. Schunk (2004), because this term addresses the active role that the individual plays in the construct of his or her understanding.

In our cognitive-oriented educational society, we too quickly overlook the relevance of the behaviorist approach to the dynamics of learning. This is no more than a reactionary instinct in response to the crude associations that this approach tends to make. But we need to remember the marked influence that behaviorist and neobehaviorist (Bigge and Shermis 2004) theories have had on our educational system. A clear example of this influence is our grading system, where we continue to work on a stimulus (grades) response (performance) basis (Santrock 2004). It is also important to recognize the initial effort of behaviorist psychologists and educators in giving the education profession a scientific character, in an early-twentieth-century academic society dominated by a rigorous observational-experimental nature (Schunk 2004).

The behaviorist theory is based precisely on observable and measurable outcomes and behaviors, where the teacher is the architect of the learning achievements of the individual. Even though some behaviorists, including B.F. Skinner, have stressed the importance of the active role that the student must play in this act of learning, Skinner (1968) is also clear about the teacher's ability to "drill" knowledge into the students. Under this model, the teacher is the central figure in learning. Environment is disregarded, and the individual fulfills a mere passive role in the acquisition of understanding. Learning under this approach is directive and external, disregarding internal locus. The following quote from Skinner (1968, 5) pretty well reflects the behaviorist view: "Left to himself in a given environment a student will learn, but he will not necessarily have been taught. The school of experience is no school at all, not because no one learns in it, but because no one teaches."

One of the basic concepts of the behaviorist approach is Edward L. Thorndike's "law of effect," which establishes how behaviors that are followed by positive outcomes will be strengthened, while behaviors followed by negative outcomes will be weakened (Santrock 2004). Thorndike is also responsible for the "trial and error" principle, which affirms how learning is gradual and occurs after the learner acquires successful responses and discards unsuccessful ones (Schunk 2004). Another of the influential precursors of the behaviorist school is Ivan Petrovich Pavlov, a Russian physiologist and pharmacologist. His work with dogs whose salivation was associated with a specific stimulus is well known in the field, and we usually refer to his work under the *classical conditioning* label. Probably the best-known behavioral psychologist is Skinner, previously mentioned, whose theory is commonly known under the term of *operant conditioning*. He expanded on the work of Thorndike and Pavlov, and under his care, we have come to extend our understanding of concepts such as reinforcement, stimulus-response, and shaping. The term *shaping* has become highly associated with the learning process, where the student is shaped or molded into the desired form or rate of behavior (Morse and Kelleher, cited in Schunk 2004).

At the other end of this learning equation, we encounter the cognitive-constructivist approach. This approach is characterized by an active role of the student, who owns the process of learning. The "learner" is primarily responsible for the construct of his or her understanding, and the teacher is only supposed to provide the learner with the environmental opportunities for the achievement of such understanding. In these theories, environment and social interaction are fundamental elements. Theories at this end of the learning continuum tend to highlight the importance of the internal processes of the individual.

An undisputed figure of this approach is the Swiss psychologist Jean Piaget. Piaget is clearly recognized as one of the precursors of constructivism (Kivinen and Ristela 2003; Sigelman and Rider 2003), even though he is most properly known for his work in cognitive development (Ormond 1995; Mayer 1987). Piaget's influence is still felt in the educational system of our times, particularly his landmark insight, the stages of cognitive development: sensorimotor, preoperational, concrete operational, and formal operational. Probably the most important contribution of these stages is their influence on how we have adapted our educational process to the gradual cognitive maturity of our children. Nonetheless, what is important for us at this point is to recognize the basic assumption behind these stages. Piaget reached his conclusion after observing how children constructed their own understanding of the world based on their experiences and their natural active exploration. This notion brings us back to the basic tenets of the cognitive-constructivist theories of learning: individuals are active learners, who construct their understanding under direct social and environmental interaction.

Social-cognitive theory

A good example of a theory that falls between the behaviorist and cognitive-constructivist approach is Albert Bandura's social-cognitive theory. Although this theory is markedly cognitive, it includes other elements beyond the mere intrinsic cognitive act of the individual that is so prominent at the cognitive-constructivist end. These elements are the person factor, the environmental events, and the behavior (Schunk 2004). In other words, the act of learning is neither solely an act of the active individual (as in the constructivist view) nor an extrinsic act residing outside the individual (as with the behaviorist view). Bandura's theory is thus a combination that includes elements of both ends of the learning spectrum.

Bandura's social-cognitive theory is also known as observational learning theory (Santrock 2004; Sigelman and Rider 2003). Under this principle, the individual learns by observing others (vicarious learning). This kind of learning is based on the concept of modeling, where the individual not only learns from the behaviors of the model but also from the consequences of the model's behaviors. If the model is praised for a given behavior, it is likely that the individual will pick up on that behavior. If, on the contrary, the same behavior punishes the model, it is likely that the learner will not repeat the behavior. The fact that the individual does not repeat the behavior does not mean that he or she failed to learn the behavior; it may well be that he or she has instead learned from the consequences of the model.

This learning is conditioned by developmental factors (Schunk 2004), an idea that remains from Piaget's cognitive developmental stages, where we cannot ask of an individual a learning task that is beyond the person's current learning capacity. Another important concept of this theory is self-efficacy, which is the learner's ability to trust him- or herself as being capable of performing a given task. Modeling of the task usually increases the learner's self-efficacy. In summary, Bandura's theory is certainly a social theory of learning. It is therefore quite significant in light of the intricate social system characteristic of Latino/a communities.

Vygotsky: A social constructivist

Lev Seminov Vygotsky was a Russian psychologist whom we can call a true constructivist. Vygotsky gave great emphasis to the capacity of the learner to construct knowledge and understanding using his or her own experiences and interactions. For Vygotsky, the function of the teacher is simply to provide the social environment that will allow the learner to develop to his or her full capacity and understanding. Knowledge is thus an internal process. This internal process is mediated by society and, more specifically, by culture (Sigelman and Rider 2003); nonetheless, it belongs to the student. The following quote from Vygotsky (1997, 48) clearly illustrates his position:

> From the scientific point of view, therefore, the assumption that the student is simply passive, just like the underestimation of his personal experience, is the greatest of sins, since it takes as foundation the false rule that the teacher is everything and the student nothing. On the contrary, . . . [the] student educates himself.

Another predominant theme in Vygotsky's theory of learning is the zone of proximal development (ZPD). This principle encourages the teacher to keep the student's tasks slightly above the student's comfort zone of learning. This is certainly a useful tool that allows the teacher to "push" the student to a level seemingly beyond his or her reach, where, guided by the teacher, the student can achieve. It is another way of propagating the environmental factors that allow the learner to construct his or her understanding.

Vygotsky's contribution to our understanding of the process of learning is significant, partly because of his inclusion of culture and cultural factors as a predominant condition of learning. He not only pointed to the social environment and interaction of the individual as an imperative of learning, but he dared to go beyond this broad approach to signal culturally specific elements that contribute to or hinder the individual's construction of understanding. We will elaborate on this point when we explore the specific cultural factors that might be affecting Latino/a education and learning.

Knowles: Andragogy

Because of Malcolm Knowles, we have come to appreciate and talk of the learning process in children and adults as being essentially different. We therefore note his effort and review the basic tenets of his andragogy (the teaching of adults). Malcolm S. Knowles, Elwood F. Holton III, and Richard A. Swanson (2005) enumerate six basic assumptions about the way adults learn:

1. *Need to know*—The adult has to have a need to know.
2. *Learner's self-concept*—Adult learners tend to associate their position as learners with being dependent, so they tend to react against the learning process. The teacher therefore needs to be able to lead the learner to exchange this dependent concept for a self-directing concept.

3. *Learner's experiences*—The teacher needs to stimulate group discussion, simulation exercises, problem-solving activities, and other resources that make use of the learner's experience.
4. *Readiness to learn*—The need to know must be timed to coincide with the developmental task of the learner.
5. *Orientation to learning*—Learning has to be life centered so as to help the learner solve problems and perform life tasks.
6. *Motivation*—The learner's motivation needs to be a mixture of internal and external drives.

POVERTY: THE MISSING LINK

There are certainly a few more theories of learning that we could mention within our effort to understand the bases of the educational system that have kept Latino/as in a marginal position. However, the aforementioned theories give us a clearer picture of the dynamics that influence our approaches to learning and education. The first issue that appears clear after reviewing these different approaches to learning is the privileged non-Latino/a position that marks the beginning of their reflections and ideas. These are Anglo-European reflections that have been imposed on us as the least favored of a system that insists on considering us foreigners.

This does not mean that the learning process of Anglo-Europeans and those of Latino/as are essentially different, nor does it mean that the learning processes of Latino/as are essentially different from those of African Americans, Indians, Africans, Asians, Pacific Islanders, and so on. At the end we are looking at human beings and their capacity to learn, appropriate, or construct knowledge. No matter how distinct we are, we all belong to the human race, so we are all endowed with the same natural capacities and abilities for learning. What makes a distinction is the condition of such a process. It is the difference in circumstances, such as cultural factors (Vygotsky), that marks the breach between learning experiences.

Among these conditions, one that we consider fundamentally important in the learning process of Latino/as is poverty. Poverty has usually been linked to the learning process as something that education is supposed to eradicate. The assumption that poverty results from a lack of education is certainly not far from reality.

But at the same time, we have failed to observe the restraints that poverty exerts as a condition of the learning environment. Even though some recent studies (see U.S. Department of Education [DOE] 2003) have included poverty as a risk factor for students, a more systematic approach to this intricate reality is still needed.

According to the Census Bureau report presented by Roberto R. Ramírez and G. Patricia de la Cruz (2002), only 26.3 percent of Latino/as in the United States earned over $35,000 a year, compared with 53.8 percent of non-Latino/a whites. The same report indicates that only 12.4 percent of Latino/as earned over $50,000 a year, compared with 31.8 percent of non-Latino/a whites. Even more alarming is the percentage of Latino/a families living under the poverty level: 14.1 percent, compared with 3.3 percent of white families and 6.6 percent of Black families sharing the poverty status (DOE 2003). It is certainly noteworthy to raise a question about our generally poor condition and our educational attainments in a learning system designed to favor the privileged.

It is here that we consider Ruby K. Payne's (2001) book *A Framework for Understanding Poverty* a breakthrough toward our comprehension of this phenomenon and its implications for learning. In her work, Payne efficiently identifies two elements we consider vital when linking poverty to lack of education. One of them is the role of language and story, and the other is the hidden rules of poverty.

Diverse studies have pointed to the role of language as a risk factor for Latino/as' education (see DOE 2003). The problem with these studies is that they tend to attribute the problem to the use of Spanish as a primary language at home while utilizing English at school. This conclusion is not only rushed but also misleading, bringing us to feel shame for what is one of our treasures and advantages: bilingual homes. The problem is much deeper and subtler than this. Payne (2001) addresses this problem of "miscommunication" as a problem of formal and casual register.

Formal register is the more elaborate speech with proper syntax used at school and work. Formal register is also the speech utilized in all standardized tests, such as SAT and ACT. In contrast, casual register is the somehow limited speech (400- to 800-word vocabulary) that tends to use incomplete syntax. Payne (2001) points to a research study done by Maria Montano-Harmon, who identifies the casual register as the common speech of minorities and poor families. This discrepancy of speech leaves the poor student at a clear disadvantage for school performance, relative to those who use formal register as a way of communication at home.

Another characteristic of formal register is its "to the point" pattern, while in casual register, we tend to beat around the bush for a while before finally getting to the point. This "story-like" speech, which is quite common for those living in poverty, becomes a handicap in a society that uses formal register and to-the-point discourse as the standard of professional communication. Moreover, this story-like speech is markedly different from the well-known story speech of beginning, plot (climax), and end. The story-like language of poverty begins with the end and revolves around a series of smaller stories that form a whole, where characters become the central point of convergence.

To this complex use of language we need to add the challenges that pose the "hidden rules" of poverty in our educational system. In her own summary, Payne (2001) addresses entertainment and relationships as the two most important elements that compose the hidden rules of poverty. In this sense, some of the most important of these hidden rules are that the ability to entertain is highly valued, the greatest possession is people (relationships), money is to be spent (especially in entertainment), the present time is the most important, and the family structure tends to be matriarchal. Of invaluable importance when reflecting on the education of Latino/as are the two elements of entertainment and relationships, because our educational system is clearly designed to separate both of these elements. Our system is sustained by production and individuality, which are clearly the antithesis of entertainment and relationships. This becomes another stumbling block in the education of our Latino/a people.

The pastoral counselor is a member of the community who, by his or her constant interaction and the nature of his or her service, has become an expert in communicating effectively with all kinds of individuals and groups. It is thus part of his or her responsibility to become aware of these and other discrepancies of communication and function, first and foremost as a "translator" for the parties involved. This first task of the pastoral counselor is a temporary task that soon meets an even more challenging route, which we call the route of awareness.

TEACHING THE LATINO/A CONDITION

Helen M. Davis (2005) made a fascinating study in which she took two groups of kindergarten students and observed in them the norms of cultural transmission of social knowledge and interaction. This study was conducted in Costa Rica, which Davis identifies as a relatively homogenous community, both ethnically and religiously. In her research, Davis chose one group from a rural-agrarian area and another from an urban-professional area. Both groups were similar in number and developmental stage in children. The teachers received special instruction, and each classroom was set to facilitate interaction through play. The rural classroom was more fit to greater interaction than the compartmentalized setting of the urban classroom, which encouraged smaller groups and independence.

Davis's hypothesis was that the rural group would become more interdependent than the urban group, reflecting the cultural and social reality of their communities. After several months of observation, her initial hunch became an overwhelming reality. The rural children manifested in their spontaneous play a clear interdependent interaction with their classmates, while the urban group clearly became more socially restricted and independent. What was even more apparent is that throughout the study, the dynamics of the groups became so natural that even the teachers departed from the initial instructions. The teachers drew closer to the sociocultural rules of their environment, which in this case reflected greater interdependence for those living in the rural area and marked independence for those living in the urban setting.

The relevance of this study is clear for our Latino/a educational experience in the United States. What we are encountering in schools, universities, and society at large is a clash of methods, strategies, and teachings that obviously is taking a toll on our Latino/a communities. As Latino/as we grew up in a highly interdependent environment where families reach beyond bloodlines and family names. This interdependent reality, commonly known as familialism or *familismo* (Marin and Marin 1991), is at the root of our Latino/a identity and has become a dominant factor in the construction of the social norms of our communities. The problem then is encountered when Latino/a students find themselves in a classroom that is encouraging a social dynamic contrary to their experience in life. Hence, we are teaching Latino/a students under an Anglo-European independent model that is only adding confusion to the already misplaced individual.

Furthermore, the idea of teaching the Latino/a condition is considered fundamentally important. This is a notion that we have borrowed from the French philosopher and educator Edgar Morin (1999), who after being assigned by UNESCO (United Nations Educational, Scientific, and Cultural Organization) to reflect on the challenges of education for the future, mentioned that the teaching of the human condition should be one of the priorities of education. We have taken the liberty of adapting his idea to talk about teaching the Latino/a condition—teaching the condition of interdependence that stands at the core of our identity, the condition of poverty and oppression that characterizes our struggles, and the condition of misunderstanding and miscommunication that seems to rob us of the opportunities to excel.

But this is not teaching that we can do by depositing information, statistics, and norms in our people. This bank education (Freire 2000) is only another way to perpetuate the educational system we are opposing. We teach the Latino/a condition by "becoming aware" of the circumstances that impress the singularity of our processes as a distinct people. This method of *conscientização* (Freire 2000)—which we have inappropriately translated as "awareness"—requires a joint effort between student and teacher in the search for understanding and knowledge. By means of this awareness, the oppressed people become acquainted with new possibilities because these new possibilities are not imposed, but born out of their own struggles. It is by awareness that individuals are able to trust their capacity to effect change in the circumstances that have kept them chained to an educational system that insists on denying them opportunities to include the culture that has enriched and shaped their lives.

We pastoral counselors become privileged participants in this process when we become active characters in the overabundance of stories of people like Juan, Maria, and Carlos. We come to realize that this is not a problem to which we can shut our eyes, continuing to ignore the devastating effect on our Latino/a people. Our commitment to justice includes a conscious commitment to denounce as prophets the unjust circumstances, and to educate our people by making them aware of the conditions that are dictating their future. By the nature of this process, our people will be able to recreate in our educational system the conditions that incorporate and validate what we are as Latino/as.

BUILDING ON HOPE

Jürgen Moltmann (2000) addresses his theology of hope and departs from the concept of promise. He uses the story of Abraham and the promise of a great nation when Sarah is childless (Genesis 12:2) as the paradigm par excellence for the meaning of hope: seeing beyond the experienced reality. The experienced reality of our Latino/a education is certainly a concern if we choose to focus merely on the statistics and the unfavorable conditions that are dictating our present. But it would not do justice to the purpose of this book and the commitment of the many people who are working hard to see beyond these conditions and hope for a better future.

The discovery of the whys, as Paulo Freire (1992) would call it, is but the beginning of a process of liberation. By becoming conscious of the conditions that keep us subjugated as a people, we are able to distance ourselves from the oppressor. Freire (1992, 48) points out the need to "localize the oppressor 'outside' [ourselves]." After this follows the task of reconstruction and the building up of hopes that will carry us through the same conditions. The call of the prophet Jeremiah was not just to destroy and pull down, but also to build. The pastoral counselor not only denounces, but also announces the capacity of the Latino/a people to overcome the obstacles we find along the road to learning and education.

We find a good example of this in the case of José and Paula, a young couple (ages thirty and twenty-eight, respectively) who immigrated to the United States from Mexico after graduating from college with bachelor's degrees in sociology six years ago. José and Paula were raised in well-to-do families, and their lives were always filled with opportunities and a vision for a future in which they would become contributors to the well-being of society. Because of unfriendly circumstances and immigration policies, they had fallen into a track of despair and hopelessness. Little by little, their dreams of professional development seemed to sink more into the "near to impossible" zone.

Only by their willingness to engage in a process of "awareness" did they become able to see and take hold of the chains and limitations keeping them from realizing their dreams. Their pastoral counselor became an instrumental part of this process by listening to their stories and constantly signaling the capacities that both of them seemed to demonstrate. This constant reminder of their strengths made them question the situation that was keeping them from continuing their education as they had planned when coming to the States. José and Paula were able to distance themselves from the conditions that limited their dreams, and in a joint effort with their pastoral counselor, they were able to find ways to continue their education. Today José is enrolled in a doctoral program at a public university, and Paula is starting her master's degree work after taking care of their child for the first four years.

José and Paula's pastoral counselor took a risk in looking beyond the conditions that were present and deciding to instill in them the hope of a different reality. This is precisely the challenge that we face as pastoral counselors seeking to work with Latino/a populations. We need to look beyond the experienced reality of despair and hopelessness and see the potential born out of the struggle of our people. Then we will be able to see bounty where others see lack, to see hope where others see despair, to see the harvest to be reaped where others see only barren soil (John 4:34-35). Aware of the struggle, we are called to build on hope.

8

A LATINO/A VIEW OF HUMAN SEXUALITY

God looked at everything he had made, and he found it very good.
Evening came, and morning followed—the sixth day.
—*Genesis 1:30 (NIV)*

God pronounces these words, taken from the book of Genesis in the Hebrew Bible, after completing the work of creation and just after creating male and female in God's image and likeness (Genesis 1:27), blessing them and commanding them to multiply and fill the earth (1:28). During the whole narrative of creation, God declares "good" the work of his creative act (verses 4, 10, 12, 18, 21, and 25), but it is only with the creation of men and women that God is willing to declare "very good" the whole of creation.

It is an interesting fact that God does not declare man and woman good on their own, but very good in relation with the rest of creation. Thus, it is in our relational nature where we reach our full potential and are able to enter into communion with God. Thinking that we can be fully human in isolation is a fallacy that stands contrary to God's plan. It is in our intimate encounter with nature, each other, and God where we fulfill God's purpose in creation, and sexuality is the primary vehicle that facilitates this purpose.

It is clear that God intended our sexual nature, since we are, among the whole of creation, the only ones designated as male and female (Genesis 1:27). Even though animals received the same command given to humans to be fertile and multiply (1:22), the sexual distinction pertains uniquely to us (Trible 1978). Our sexuality is no mistake; God intended us to be sexual beings—and sexual beings beyond the mere act of procreation common to the animal kingdom and us. In light of this plan of God, we can declare with God that, contrary to what we may have been taught, our sexuality is one more of the gifts that God bountifully bestows on us. And if we are fair, we need to recognize that it is not just one more gift, it is a special gift, a gift that makes us stand apart from the whole of creation, a gift that makes us unique, loved, and cherished in God's eyes.

Since the word *sexuality* is a loaded word that tends to be misinterpreted because of the prejudices that it awakens, it is very important that we agree on a common conceptualization of the meaning pursued with such a word. For this purpose R. R. Prada (1992) affirms that sexuality goes beyond genitalia. A truthful sexual education reaches beyond the mere biological and mechanical aspects of sex, in order to explore the psychological, cultural, and spiritual aspects that make of the same a truly human richness. Sexuality is then a holistic term that includes some of the most important aspects of our human interactions, and this term cannot be reduced to a lonesome biological aspect that, although important and thoroughly considered in this chapter, does not constitute the totality of what sexuality entails.

LATINO/A FUNCTIONS OF SEXUALITY

In a recent book (Montilla 2004), three different functions of sexuality that we consider fundamental when trying to understand the Latino/a view of human sexuality are addressed: the procreative (reproductive), relational, and recreational functions of sexuality. These three functions are interrelated, and a good balance among them constitutes the mark for a healthy sexual relationship between partners. Nevertheless, these three functions of sexuality are independent and can easily appear in a given relationship without each other. For instance, it is quite common to encounter couples who enjoy the recreational and relational nature of sex but are not open to its procreative aspect. Likewise, it is not unusual to find couples who are open to and seeking the procreative quality of sex but do not find pleasure or intimacy during intercourse. Finally, the relational, intimate nature of sex is often enjoyed, sought, and needed by persons with biological and psychological disorders who are not otherwise able to conduct pleasurable or reproductive intercourse.

Contrary to what one may think, these three functions of our sexuality are rooted in scriptural teachings. This may come as a surprise, since in our Christian worldview, the reproductive function of sexuality was the only one encouraged and sometimes the only one taught. This notion is quite different from the Hebrew take on sexuality. Even though the procreative function of sexuality remained the primary and foremost nature of sexual intercourse, the pleasurable and relational aspects also were highly regarded by the people of Israel.

Moreover, the motives to uphold the procreative function of sexuality in its primordial place are quite different in the two religious interpretations. In the Hebrew worldview, procreation was equated with eternal life. It was by having children that one remained present in the minds, thoughts, and narratives of the people; it was by the carrying on of a name and a story that one remained immortal and present. This was the main reason why being sterile was considered a curse and also the reason for the prohibition of same-sex sexual relationships. The understanding of everlasting life is quite different in our Christian theology, which has a very different idea of the value of the procreative function of sexuality.

In our Christian mentality, honoring God's command to "be fertile and multiply" (Genesis 1:28 NAB) is simply a duty, an obligation tainted with the shameful process of sexual enjoyment. This is the reasoning that has encouraged some of our Christian theologians, including Thomas Aquinas, to say that enjoying the sexual act is a sin, even if the intent is merely to procreate.

Besides the aforementioned text of Genesis 1:27, we have become familiar with the prohibition text of Leviticus 18 and 20 as the other biblical text that explicitly talks about sexual behavior. These two chapters of the Hebrew Bible address the various forbidden forms of intercourse and the penalties applicable to those who infringe upon these prohibitions. Among them we have incest, uncleanness (due to intercourse during menstruation), male-to-male intercourse, and bestiality. It is interesting that among the sexual prohibitions we find a reference to idolatry (Leviticus 18:21), since this concept of idolatry as a sin is strongly linked to the sexual nature. This concept was carried forward in the New Testament writings.

Another important consideration is noticed by Ilona Rashkow (2000), who highlights the lack of reference to lesbianism despite the clear reference to homosexuality (male-to-male intercourse) in Leviticus 18:22. We witness a similar situation in New Testament writings, where male-to-male intercourse is specifically mentioned (Romans 1:27; 1 Corinthians 6:9), while that is not the case in reference to female-to-female intercourse. There is but one reference, in Romans 1:26, to women and unnatural relations, but the text is not clear to what *unnatural* might mean. In any case, the Leviticus text is used in conjunction with the Romans and Corinthians texts to continue and accentuate the idea of the shameful, sinful, and disgraceful state of sexual intercourse. As a result, we have been robbed of the abundance of blessings received through our sexuality. Raymond J. Lawrence (1989) points out that in the Hebrew tradition, sexuality was highly valued as a key component of the human experience. It is in the best interest of pastoral counselors to recover a more biblical and positive view of sexuality.

The pleasurable function of human sexuality has been one of those blessings that throughout our Christian history has been looked upon with suspicion. But if we observe carefully, we find passages in the Hebrew Bible that refer to the recreational nature of sexuality. The first of these passages is in Genesis 18:12, which reports that after Abraham and Sarah were told they were to have a child, despite their advanced age, Sarah pronounces the following words: "Now that I am so withered and my husband is so old, am I still to have sexual pleasure?"

Her words give a clear indication of the spontaneous and natural association of sexual intercourse with a pleasurable act. Another such text is found in Deuteronomy 24:5, where the author talks about the laws that govern marriage and mentions the exception given from military duty to those newly married so the husband can bring "joy" to the wife. The law of *onah*, which refers to the sexual duty of a man to a woman (Exodus 21:7-10) indicates that the man has to provide three things to his woman: clothes, food, and sexual pleasure. Men were required to observe *onah* during pregnancy and lactation, which shows the importance of the recreational aspect of sex. Rabbis interpret the meaning of *onah* to be not only quantity of sex, but quality as well.

An even more explicit text is found in Proverbs 5:18-19 (JPS): "Let your fountain be blessed; Find joy in the wife of your youth—A loving doe, a graceful mountain goat. Let her breasts satisfy you at all times; be infatuated with love of her always." Similar pleasure-inspired texts are found in the Song of Songs 4:9-11 and 5:2-4, among others.

As we can easily observe, the recreational function of sexuality is well regarded in Hebrew mentality—and not only well regarded, but encouraged and expected within sexual intercourse. It is then an unsound partial interpretation of the scriptures that constitutes the real problem, a problem that reaches beyond the sexual quality of our beings to include issues related to our image and self-esteem. By denying our sexuality, we are denying the wisdom of God in creating us as sexual beings. We are affirming that God made a mistake while giving us organs such as the clitoris, whose only function is to bring pleasure to the woman.

We equate ourselves with a defective product, and in doing so, we depreciate the worth that God bestows on us as stewards of God's creation. We distort our image and open the doors to feelings such as incompetence and unworthiness, feelings that leave us in a compromising position and often lead us to remain silent against injustice and oppression. This promotes the belief that, since we are not worthy, we deserve the wrong of others. Since we are a mistake, we do not deserve God's love but God's pity. We end up wounded, fragile, and unable to fulfill the task that God entrusted to us at the time of creation. The repercussions of such a view are clear, and it is time that we, as pastoral counselors, begin to facilitate a change in the framework that helps us read our sexual nature through a different perspective.

Finally, concerning the relational function of our sexuality, we notice in the verses in Genesis our intrinsic relational nature, which was inherited in creation and where we received our worth in connection with the rest of creation. We observe this relational nature basically at two levels: with each other and with creation. We were created to be in relationship with self, others, nature, and God. It is interesting to notice that in the second story of creation, God created man and then created the animals as companions. To complete the circle and web of life, God created a person with a higher vision, an *Ezer Kenegdo* (equally powerful helper), the woman.

Nature is an ally, a source of strength and joy, an always selfless partner willing to share with us in its beauty and colorfulness, and finally, a constant witness of God's love for God's creation. Nature is a channel to God and a special vehicle that many writers have used to understand and get closer to the Creator. Nature is also a spiritual path that makes us look with wonder and awe at God's power, wisdom, and compassion.

The second level of this relational function of our sexuality is connected with our intimacy with each other. This intimacy is either individual or collective, and is marked by mutuality and participation. Since the goal of an intimate encounter is to achieve "oneness," the goal of each partner should be to invest fully in the achievement of this purpose. This oneness is rooted in the biblical idea of a man and a woman becoming one (Genesis 2:24), which is an idea that communicates to us our need for relationship with others.

In isolation we are incomplete, and it is only by reaching out to another (partner, community, God) that we can become a complete unit. In this sense, we can say that prayer becomes a sexual act in which we are able to communicate and become intimate with God. Conversely, the sexual act can be considered a form of prayer when intimacy is purposefully sought between partners.

The word *intimacy* is an often-misunderstood term. Because of the taboo status that we have given to the word *sex*, some of our Latino/a people have come to think of sexual intercourse as being the only type of intimacy. It is true that the sexual encounter between partners represents an intimate act. However, the word *intimacy* refers to a much broader spectrum of behaviors and encounters, most of them not even physical. This suggests a real problem for our Latino/a population, inasmuch as we continue avoiding a direct encounter with the blessing of our sexuality, and by doing so, we reduce the rich concept of intimacy to a mere euphemism.

The pastoral counselor working with Latino/as has to be aware of this reality and be willing to make a contractual agreement that allows and encourages Latino/a consultees to use direct and proper discourse. The counselor needs to exemplify this by calling things by name (sex, penis, vagina, etc.) in a natural manner devoid of any malice and shame. It is also the task of the pastoral counselor to foster a renewed understanding of intimacy, especially when working with Latino/a couples and families. We do this by inviting our consultees to think of intimacy as a broader concept that encompasses many different aspects. We can call this the task of reconstructing Latino/a intimacy.

RECONSTRUCTING LATINO/A INTIMACY

Dennis A. Bagarozzi (2001) has observed seven different aspects of intimacy that are commonly encountered within couples. Sexual intimacy is just but one of these seven aspects, indicating that although primordial, it exists in relation with several different elements that constitute the basis for a healthy relationship. These seven aspects of intimacy are emotional, psychological, intellectual, sexual, physical, spiritual, and aesthetic intimacy. Each one of these contains elements that are important for us to consider and apply when working with Latino/as.

Emotional intimacy

The first aspect of intimacy, emotional intimacy, indicates the capacity, ability, and openness to share feelings between partners. This is an essential characteristic of good communication of the couple, the family, and the community. The language of feelings allows individuals to communicate at a level that, although initially threatening, becomes less defensive and invites to deeper understanding. Individuals who are able to communicate and express their feelings and emotions are regularly more willing to step outside themselves and consider the other's position. It is also important to consider that the expression of feelings is implicitly associated with vulnerability, and some individuals may resist communicating at this level, as a result possibly appearing emotionally unavailable. Part of the pastoral counselor's duty is to encourage and sometimes train partners to openly express and recognize feelings.

Psychological intimacy

The next aspect, psychological intimacy, results from the individual need to validate meaning by sharing one's hopes, dreams, desires, fantasies, doubts, and problems with another human being. This is a form of intimacy that can be greatly utilized by the pastoral counselor while helping Latino/a consultees. Our Latino/a culture is basically born out of dreams and fantasies that are usually communicated within our oral traditions.

The power of stories to communicate meaning is commonly utilized in Latino/a communities. Having this in mind, the pastoral

counselor might want to use narrative techniques that permit partners to explore the possibility of inviting their partner into their
emotional world. This can be offered as a type of playful interaction where it is acceptable to be silly and adventurous, qualities
that fare well with Latino/a idiosyncrasies.

Intellectual intimacy

The term *intellectual intimacy* refers mainly to the sharing of ideas,
thoughts, and beliefs. Respect is a fundamental principle that
needs to be observed at this level of intimacy, since intellectual
communication is founded on a basic trust to be understood and
supported. Although the person's worldview is subject to the challenge it may encounter with another, this needs to be a gradual
challenge that allows the person to grow slowly as his or her ideas
change shape. A sudden attack might become confusing and pro-
voke unfavorable reactions in either partner.

It is important to invite couples and families to designate a
safe zone (place, time, day, etc.) where this intellectual exchange
is encouraged. Providing rules that the couple or family can use
in this zone could be an excellent task in which the pastoral counselor might serve as mediator. The idea behind this is to give the
couple or family a specific space in their lives to nurture and connect with each other intellectually. While helping to provide the
rules for this space, it is important to consider the defensiveness
that intellectual sharing tends to elicit within individuals. Thus,
the pastoral counselor has an important role as a participant in the
composition of these rules.

Sexual intimacy

The fourth of the intimacy aspects mentioned by Bagarozzi (2001)
is sexual intimacy. The achievement of intimacy at this level comes
from numerous elements, including thoughts, feelings, desires, and
fantasies of a sexually explicit nature that contribute to the sexual
arousal between partners. This is a very significant ingredient of sexual intercourse that couples tend to neglect. The idea of *verguenza*
(shame) so common for Latino/a individuals heavily contributes
to intensifying this barrier to sexual intimacy. As we noticed before,
the idea of shame is strongly linked with the religious understanding of sexuality inherited in our Latino/a communities. Since the

pastoral counselor is usually anointed with some sort of religious authority, it is within his or her power to offer a healthier religious framework that incites couples to invest in this romantic foreplay of sexual intimacy.

Bagarozzi (2001) also mentions physical closeness and bodily contact as a central component of the act of conjugal love. Kisses, hugs, massages, and physical touch with arousal purposes are also part of this physical closeness needed to achieve pleasurable intercourse. The pastoral counselor working with Latino/a populations will also be able to encourage couples to try different sexual positions that may bring more pleasure to the sexual activity. Considering that Latino homes tend to be formed by larger families than those of non-Latino/a whites (Therrien and Ramírez 2001) as part of their daily living, it is a good idea to encourage couples to explore the possibility of frequent getaways that allow them to have a more private environment, which in turn might lead them to more satisfactory sexual performance. In view of the economic constraints on many of our Latino/a families, the pastoral counselor needs to present this idea as an investment in the well-being of the family. Moreover, he or she might want to prepare some economic suggestions (hotel/resort promotions, retreat opportunities, camping trips, etc.).

Pastoral counselors could use Robert Sternberg's (1996) views on love as including passion, intimacy, and commitment. The passionate love, the burning desire for the other, is not a specific event, but rather a process that unfolds throughout the day with words and deeds that reveal to the other the desire, absorption, and ecstasy that are to come. Committed love implies an active role of both partners to keep the life of the relationship invigorated.

Physical intimacy

The fifth aspect to be considered in a healthy relationship is physical intimacy, referring to nonsexual touch. The importance of touch is widely recognized and reaches beyond the intimate life of the couple. For instance, William H. Masters and Virginia E. Johnson (1975) mention several research studies in which touch became the difference between life and death for newborn infants. Nowadays this is widely accepted as fact, and most hospitals have instituted programs in their neonatal units where volunteers are recruited and trained to provide infants with the much-needed developmental element of physical touch. It is also quite common to hear about the "healing touch," especially for hospital or hospice patients, who are often deprived of such a fundamental human need.

Within the life of the couple and the life of the family, there are many ways in which this physical touch can be encouraged. Bagarozzi (2001) mentions some, including holding hands, cuddling together, dancing, and nonsexual massages. Usually Latino/a individuals are very good at practicing this form of intimacy, and in our Latino/a culture, touch is not just relegated to partners or family. In a study conducted by Sidney M. Jourard in 1966 (reported in Morreale, Spitzberg, and Barge 2001), couples were observed in casual conversations in coffee shops for a period of one hour. During this period of time, couples in San Juan, Puerto Rico, touched on 180 occasions, those in Paris, France, touched 110 times, couples in Gainesville, Florida, touched only twice, and those in London, England, did not touch at all. Sherwyn P. Morreale, Brian H. Spitzberg, and J. Kevin Barge (2001) also quote another, more recent study that renders similar results. In conclusion, touch is a predominant factor in the life of our Latino/a communities and one that assures us a healthy physical intimacy for the most part.

Spiritual intimacy

During the last few years, therapists have revisited the concept of spiritual intimacy with renewed interest. Bagarozzi (2001) mentions components of this sharing of thoughts, feelings, and beliefs of a spiritual nature. Among them we have the sharing of moral values, the meaning of existence, life after death, and the nature of our personal relationship with God. Seemingly, this is an aspect of intimacy that should not present much of a problem for the couple or the family, but in reality it tends to be a source of controversy, especially for individuals inclined toward fundamentalism who do not give other members of the family an opportunity to form and express their own spiritual opinions.

As pastoral counselors, we are usually expected to address spiritual intimacy. This certainly gives us an advantage over secular counselors, who might be afraid to compromise their position by entering such delicate terrain. But this is precisely the nature of our authority in this field and could contribute to problems while counseling. It is quite common to feel a need to preach, teach, and many times impose our own assumptions, ideas, and beliefs on our consultees. Even more problematic is that our Latino/a people often expect and many times demand this dynamic. The pastoral counselor needs to be especially aware of this danger so he or she can allow a free and unbiased exchange of ideas among partners and/or family members.

Aesthetic intimacy

Finally, we have aesthetic intimacy, which as the name conveys, is about sharing personally moving experiences, uplifting or moti vating ideas and thoughts, and awe-inspiring situations, events, places, and information. We encounter this aspect of intimacy in social and recreational interactions like going to a park, a lake, or a beach, as well as participating in a cultural event like a play, a concert, or an opera, or in outings to the movies, the bowling alley, a nice restaurant, a coffee shop, and so forth. Since the family is such a primordial part of the life of the Latino/a (Santiago-Rivera, Arredondo, and Gallardo-Cooper 2002; Falicov 1998; Smith and Montilla 2005), many of these activities are planned and carried through mostly as community or family events.

Here the pastoral counselor needs to be watchful to avoid imposing Euro-American standards that reduce this kind of intimacy only to the life of the couple. Nonetheless, these activities might be suggested as couple-only activities to celebrate special moments in the life of the couple (for example, anniversaries or professional accomplishments). But for the most part, the counselor needs to be aware that these are often going to be family- and/or community-driven events.

Time for intimacy

A common denominator of these different types of intimacy is the time factor. Couples and families need to take time aside for themselves. This time aside is a time away from situational distractions such as the television, the phone, the pager, and in general the day-to-day nuisances that impede communication and therefore connection between partners and families. This is especially important for Latino/as, because of the collectivism and the need to improve the health of the community. Reframing the negative concept of sexuality that has been part of our Christian heritage is a very positive way to initiate this openness within Latino/a communities, openness that can become the foundation for a more intimate life of the couple and the family.

MODELS OF SEXUAL AROUSAL

As pastoral counselors, we are called to propose a more positive view of human sexuality within our Latino/a communities. Therefore, it is important to understand the basic tenets of sexual response and arousal as presented by the scientific community. We offer a brief summary with the goal of giving you some basic facts that will help broaden your perspective regarding the beautiful gift of sexuality that our loving God has bestowed on us. We hope that this exposition will create in you a desire that will drive you to inquire deeper into this theme and at the same time equip you with basic language that you may need to use in your professional practice.

Before we mention the basic models of sexual arousal, it is important that we understand the biological process that we identify as such. Usually, when we mention sexual arousal, the picture that comes to our minds is the physical excitement that is characterized by the erection of the penis in males and the swelling and lubrication of the female vagina. What escapes from the basic observation of this complicated process is that many other factors form part of a person's sexual arousal. There are psychological and endocrinal as well as physical components (Miracle, Miracle, and Baumeister 2003) that play a part in this sexual symphony. The brain becomes responsible for awakening desires, thoughts, fantasies, and memories, as well as processing all the external information that responds to touch, visual stimulation, and so on. Our endocrine system teems with higher levels of testosterone in males and estrogens in females. And finally our genitals play their part by becoming ready for direct sexual stimulation. Together, they all form a wonderful biological maneuver that gives testimony to the magnificence of our Creator.

The classic model of sexual arousal is called the EPOR model and was suggested by the gynecologist Masters and the psychologist Johnson (1961, 1966, 1970, 1976) who, in the tradition of Alfred Kinsey (1948), conducted extensive research and published their studies on human sexuality. The EPOR model is composed of four different phases: excitement, plateau, orgasmic, and resolution. The excitement phase is characterized by increased flow of blood to the genitalia, which results in the erection of muscle tissue including the nipples, the penis, and the vagina, as well as lubrication of the vagina. The plateau phase is the advanced state of arousal that precedes orgasm. This phase is characterized by the increased size of the testes in males and by the swelling of the outer vagina in females. The clitoris shortens and withdraws in females. Then we have the orgasmic phase and, finally, the resolution phase, in which the body returns to the pre-arousal state. Robert Crooks and Karla Baur (2005) caution against simplifying and using these phases as a mere checklist, since that could obscure the richness of individual variation and the diverse ways of experiencing sex.

Another well-known model of sexual arousal is Helen Singer Kaplan's model (1979), which has three phases instead of four. Moreover, the Kaplan model explains each phase as an independent unit that does not function in a sequential manner. These three phases are desire, excitement, and orgasm (Miracle, Miracle, and Baumeister 2003; Greenberg, Bruess, and Haffner 2002). The importance of this model is that it makes desire an independent element. This in turn constitutes a very important condition, since the most common sexual problems are related to lack of desire. This was initially thought to supply the deficiencies of the Masters and Johnson model of sexual arousal. However, Roy J. Levin (2002) points out that desire is not necessarily required for sexual expression, and many people engage in sexual activity although they initially may have no desire; as the encounter progresses and the body responds, satisfaction is then experienced.

SEXUAL DISORDERS

Sexual difficulties are complex and have a multifactorial origin that includes physiological, psychological, sociological, cultural, and contextual as well as spiritual factors. As mentioned before, the most commonly reported sexual problem is the lack of desire, technically called hypoactive sexual desire (*Diagnostic and Statistical Manual [DSM]* 2000). Among the biological factors that contribute to this lack of desire, we find menopause, nerve damage, diabetes, heart disease, smoking, obesity, medications (including antidepressants), and decrease in hormonal fluctuations. Some of the psychological factors that contribute to this disorder are stress, depression, past sexual abuse, poor body image, and history of unsatisfactory relationships (Miracle, Miracle, and Baumeister 2003). Another form of the disorder of desire is sexual aversion, which is characterized by disgust at the idea of a sexual encounter.

Another group of sexual disorders is known as sexual arousal disorders (*DSM* 2000). Among these, the male erectile disorder is reported with most frequency. The erectile disorder consists of the male's inability to achieve and/or sustain erections for a period of time that would allow him to complete sexual activity. Pastoral counselors need to be aware that it is quite normal for a healthy man to report erectile problems. Such problems are usually due to one or a combination of the following factors: stress, fatigue, alcohol consumption, and short-term illness (Miracle, Miracle, and Baumeister 2003).

Finally, we have orgasmic disorders, such as premature ejaculation in males, the inability to experience orgasm or female orgasmic disorder in females, and sexual pain disorders. Even though our job might not be to treat these disorders, to the best of our capacity we need to be able to recognize them and refer our consultees to the proper clinical help. Also, we need to encourage healthier lifestyles in our Latino/a populations so these disorders can be avoided.

Sexuality is about connection with self, others, nature, and God. Sexuality and spirituality pursue the same goal: intimacy, equality, companionship, mutuality, and sense of community. As spiritual beings trying to be humans, we thirst for this connection. Issues of power, dominion, competence, and individual achievement have no room in a satisfactory, enriching, empowering, and loving relationship. Although this might sound idealistic, as pastoral counselors we can invite our Latino/a consultees to work toward that, knowing that God has equipped us with whatever is necessary to achieve this level of intimacy.

9

CARING FOR THE FAMILY

There are two main scenarios in which a pastoral counselor would be called upon to assist Latino families: consultations and crises. The most widely recognized of these two is the family consultation, accepted by both the family and the counselor as a time of exploration and treatment of family issues. This family consultation encompasses a treatment plan, a contractual agreement between both parties (stating goals of therapy, number of sessions, etc.), and a specific time set apart for the sole purpose of family counseling. In secular counseling, this is basically the idea of family therapy, but that is not the case for the pastoral counselor. Within the paradigm of consultation, the Latino family interprets the pastoral counselor as being a sojourner with them in resolving the identified concern, someone with whom they will join together in overcoming the adversity. *Respeto* from the pastoral counselor is expected and given and further enhances the bond necessary to develop a working and successful relationship.

Besides providing this classical form of intervention for families, the pastoral counselor is called to serve and minister to families undergoing severe stressful events due to traumas, deaths, and crises. Even though these events are considered and studied as part of crisis intervention techniques, we believe that the role of the pastoral counselor is fundamentally different from the one played by the crisis intervener. Because of his or her godly association, the pastoral counselor primarily represents and reminds family members of the presence of God in their time of distress. This is almost an automatic response, but it does not guarantee a successful intervention. There are family dynamics that need to be observed in order to promote a healthy channeling of emotions without meddling with the process. Moreover, the job of the pastoral counselor in the midst of these stressful family events reaches beyond the limitations associated with crisis intervention because of our availability and promptness of assistance, witnessing not only the event resolution but also on many occasions the event itself.

It is also important to consider that many of these stressful events do not strictly qualify as a crisis. Crisis, as defined by Albert

R. Roberts (2000, 7), is "a period of psychological disequilibrium, experienced as a result of a hazardous event or situation that constitutes a significant problem that cannot be remedied by using familiar coping strategies." In this sense, although a death is a traumatic event, it may not represent a crisis for a particular family. Similarly, a diagnosis of cancer might be just one of the multiple dreadful diagnoses that an individual has received, so it might not represent a crisis but does represent a distressful event. Losing a job after being in and out of several jobs in the last six months might not qualify as a crisis, but again, it might not be that easy after all.

In this sort of event, the help of a crisis intervener would be almost irrelevant, while the support offered by a pastoral counselor is decisive. It is therefore the purpose of this chapter to enhance and facilitate the role of the pastoral counselor in both consultations and crises, especially emphasizing the participation of the counselor in families' distressful events, since that kind of situation is frequently neglected in crisis intervention training and family counseling training.

The Rodriguez family provides a good example of distressful family events that call for care and support from the pastoral counselor. Tomas is a fifty-two-year-old immigrant from Peru, who arrived in the United States eighteen years ago and, after completing a medical specialty in internal medicine, was able to build a prosperous practice that gained him and his family much respect and economic stability. Tomas married Linda, who is two years younger than he, and whom he identifies as his high school sweetheart. Linda, a medical doctor in her country of origin, decided to trade her profession for the real estate business, where she became a successful entrepreneur. They have three children: Jorge Alberto, the oldest, is twenty-two and in his senior year of pre-med school at Baylor University, in Waco, Texas; Teresa, the middle child, born in the States seventeen years ago and currently finishing her last year of high school, is the academic prodigy of the family and is currently pursuing her graduation with valedictorian honors. Junior is the youngest at only fourteen years of age and the closest child to Tomas. Life for Tomas has not been easy, but he considers himself fortunate because after a malfunction of his kidneys twelve years ago, he was able to find a compatible donor after only a couple of months in dialysis. Sadly for Tomas and his family, this kidney is already giving up, and he is back at the hospital, expecting to be subjected once again to what he calls the "martyrdom of dialysis," at least until he is able to find another suitable donor.

Since the Rodriguez family faced a similar situation before, we can assume they have already gathered some coping mechanisms to confront this new challenge. We also need to consider that the "surprise factor" does not play a role in their ordeal, since the life of a transplanted kidney averages around ten years, and both Tomas and Linda, with their extensive medical knowledge, were expecting this.

In light of these considerations, we can affirm that this scenario is more of a distressful event than a crisis, at least for Linda and Tomas. The response of the children might be quite different, inasmuch as Teresa and Junior were too young to have assimilated the previous impact of Tomas's chronic condition. Junior's potential reaction is a real matter of concern because of his age and his closeness to Tomas, but the parents say they have been preparing their children for this time. Although suggested by their priest, the family has rejected the idea of counseling, at least for the present moment. The pastoral counselor who functions as a trained clinical chaplain at the hospital was then contacted by the priest, who informed him of the situation and asked him to be attentive to the needs of the Rodriguez family.

INITIAL CONSIDERATIONS

When working with Latino/a families, the first and foremost premise must be to understand the diversity of the Latino/a population (Arredondo and Pérez 2003; Casas, Vásquez, and Ruiz De Esparza 2002; Santiago-Rivera, Arredondo, and Gallardo-Cooper 2002; Smith and Montilla 2005). It is but an illusion to attempt to enclose Latino/as within the phenotypes of a sole racial group. The Latino/a appearance is composed of many faces and many colors. Our identity is as varied as our culture, food, music, and customs inherited from Africans, Europeans, and our indigenous people. There are black Latino/as, white Latino/as, mestizo Latino/as, and those in between these categories. Even within families, there are different skin colors (Falicov 1998).

The pastoral counselor looking to work with Latino families needs to be aware of this diversity and forget about stereotypes that depict Latino/as as one homogeneous group. Furthermore, this diversity reaches beyond racial identity and extends to educational level, socioeconomic status, and religious affiliation. Moreover, Herbert Goldenberg and Irene Goldenberg (2002) add to the counselor's checklist the generational level, the acculturation level, the languages spoken, and the one language preferred (Santiago-Rivera, Arredondo, and Gallardo-Cooper 2002), as well as the adherence to cultural values shown by the family. It is not a simple task to regard this array of details, but we can start working our way through them by avoiding cultural or racial generalizations.

It is of great importance to highlight the value of the family institution within the Latino/a culture. Among the diversity of our customs, traditions, and values, the role of the family as a primordial establishment of our social composition remains at the core of our Latino/a identity. Family as the primary teaching tool of community dynamics represents the overall picture of a people driven by a communitarian spirit. Family is not just family for our Latino/a people. It extends beyond the ties of bloodline to reach the *compadres* and *comadres* (godparents) and even friends without any particular connection with the family. This phenomenon, known as *familismo* (Marin and Marin 1991; Bridgers et al. 1997; Vega 1995; Cauce and Domenech-Rodriguez 2002), denotes the marked interdependence of our Latino/a people.

Family is not merely a decorative establishment; it fulfills several practical functions that help in the survival task of its individuals. One of these functions is the provision of economic resources. Investing in people is one of the values encouraged within the Latino/a family system. Historically, people have remained more valuable than money in an economic system prone to fluctuate within the finances of the family. In this sense, children have also been regarded as a source of income, since they are expected to contribute to the family finances whenever possible. In exchange, parents are responsible to help children even after they have gained financial independence (Sue and Sue 2003). This financial obligation has certainly decreased (Santiago-Rivera, Arredondo, and Gallardo-Cooper 2002), especially in more-acculturated Latino/a families; nonetheless it represents a marked characteristic of the Latino/a family functioning.

A second practical function of the Latino arrangement of family is to offer emotional support (Vega 1995; Goldenberg and

Goldenberg 2002). Latino/as are expected first and foremost to solve their problems or find the needed support at times of distress within the boundaries of the family. The help of a counselor should not be enlisted unless all the family resources have proved to be insufficient. This attitude, linked to the principle of honor within the family, embodies one of the primary blocks to the counselor's efforts (Bridgers et al. 1997). Nonetheless, the savvy pastoral counselor will be able to recognize this family interdependence as a source of strength and support that needs to be commended and, if possible, enhanced.

A counselor who lacks sufficient knowledge of the concept of *familismo* frequently misunderstands this interdependence at the root of our Latino/a identity. Labels such as *enmeshed* or *codependent* are readily available to describe the dynamics exposed in the Latino/a family (Santiago-Rivera, Arredondo, and Gallardo-Cooper 2002). As signaled by Goldenberg and Goldenberg (2002), this exemplifies the danger of imposing Euro-American, middle-class standards and values upon the experience of Latino/a communities. Only by awareness of our own biases will we as pastoral counselors be able to suspend ethnocentric attitudes and behavior, thus enhancing the therapeutic effort.

Finally, it is important to mention the role of "family rituals" within the reality of *familismo*. Celia Jaes Falicov (1998) suggests that the interdependent Latino family is rich in symbolism that illustrates several values emphasized under this communitarian worldview. "Solidarity, family pride, loyalty, and a sense of belonging and obligation to one's blood ties" (p. 163) are all reflected in the different rituals enacted frequently, especially among middle-class Latino/as. Rituals are another form of intimacy that the pastoral counselor needs to foster, especially among those who, because of the circumstances, have settled with being content with a life of disconnectedness.

One more important consideration while working with Latino families is the concept of *personalismo* (Flores 2000; Bridgers et al. 1997; Cauce and Domenech-Rodriguez 2002). This concept requires the establishment of a personal relationship before undertaking a particular task. In other words, the relationship needs to be formed before you proceed with the counseling dialogue. In terms of pastoral counseling, we talk about being anointed before we can minister to the individual or, in this case, the family. Considering the Rodriguez case, the pastoral counselor has been contacted by the family priest and is called to minister to a family unknown to him or her. Thus, he or she is a stranger to the family, making it difficult to achieve trust.

In the parable of the good shepherd, Jesus enumerates the characteristics of the shepherd, and among these characteristics, he mentions knowing the sheep by name (John 10:4). In the Hebrew mentality, to name something is to know something. This is the significance of why Adam and Eve were given the power to name everything on earth (Genesis 2:19-20). This is the same reason we were entrusted as stewards and stewardesses of God's creation (Psalm 8). Finally, it is the reason that forbids us to use the name of God in vain (Exodus 20:7) because we name that which is under our dominion. We could certainly say that a good pastor (shepherd) knows his or her sheep by name, knows about their problems and difficulties, knows about their joys, knows about their families, and their hopes. This pastor knows them! However, in our example, the situation of the pastoral counselor is a bit different; even though he knows their names (Tomas, Linda, Jorge Alberto, Teresa, and Junior), he does not know what it is happening to them, where they are emotionally and spiritually, what their worries and hopes are. He is not their shepherd. It is only by building a relationship, by building rapport—or as Suzanne Midori Hanna and Joseph H. Brown (1999) call it, by joining—that we are granted the authority to initiate a therapeutic exchange.

Although some pastoral counselors serve full-time as pastors, it is guaranteed that their therapeutic services will be demanded by sheep of another corral, sheep that do not recognize their voice as the one of the shepherd (John 10:4). It is then imperative to stress the necessity of building a relationship with the family as the counselor's initial task, at least at this stage. Stating name and purpose of visit, being cordial and respectful, recognizing every member of the family, and greeting them all amiably are but a few of the elements that can guarantee a successful intervention. Body language also is important. Conserving a demeanor appropriate to the situation, maintaining eye contact, assuming the same eye level as the person speaking, using appropriate gestures, and observing an appropriate distance are elements that the pastoral counselor can add to the list of available resources while caring for Latino/a families.

Finally, the initial considerations to be observed by the pastoral counselor should include honor and *respeto*. Goldenberg and Goldenberg (2002) mention honor and respect as a motive of pride for parents within Latino/a families. Raising respectful children and saving the honor of the family are considered moral obligations for the members of the family. Breaking the limitations imposed by these two highly regarded values is comparable to professional suicide. One of the important tasks of the counselor is then to identify the appointed leader of the family and to offer him or her the due respect of his or her role. Recognizing each member of the family and addressing them directly encourages participation and strengthens the joining process. Finally, allowing the family to "save face" when confronted with issues they are not ready to discuss completes the set of therapeutic tools that shield the honor and respect so important to the Latino/a family.

To prepare for meeting the Rodriguez family, the pastoral counselor will need to memorize names. During the initial exchange, he will be attentive to the verbal and nonverbal dynamics that allow one to identify assumed roles of the family members. Is there an appointed family spokesperson? Is this spokesperson delegated or self-appointed? If delegated, who is silently in charge? Is the participation of the family members sequential and organized, or disrupted and disorganized? While gathering and processing all these details, the pastoral counselor invites the family to state the problem as if he is not totally aware of the situation. Inquiring about a precipitating event, previous similar events, and means of coping at that time will also generate important data that the pastoral counselor must identify in order to discern the strengths of the family.

Likewise, it is essential to identify family stressors, both expected and unexpected (Gladding 2002), and intervention plans that can be offered as therapy continues. This is the process that Hanna and Brown (1999) refer to as hypothesizing. Finally, the pastoral counselor will be able to identify sources of emotional support in addition to the present members of the family (for example, priest, friends, and extended family).

With all these tools at hand, the pastoral counselor can contemplate a map to follow, although we believe that by this time, much good may have already been done. Bernard L. Bloom (1981) affirms that about two-thirds of persons who receive single-session therapy talk about being helped by that one-time visit with the therapist. Time constraints are prevalent characteristics of the pastoral counselor intervention in distressful family events. Under these circumstances, there is either one extended visit (two hours or more) or repetitive short visits for a prolonged period of time (two to three weeks). The one-and-a-half-hour visit of family therapy once or twice a week is rather unusual. Likewise, the inability to take notes represents another challenge that needs to be considered. In the midst of these distressful events, it is unfitting to be seen taking notes. This is why it is extremely important to memorize the referral information (Hanna and Brown 1999). Both written and orally communicated information are equally important to consider before the first interview. The pastoral counselor has to minister one visit at a time.

THE NEW FACE OF THE LATINO/A FAMILY

The Latino family is facing new social dynamics that are changing its outlook. The traditional Latino family—many years of marriage and a large number of children where everyone remains together—is time after time being put to the test. Ana Mari Cauce and Melanie Domenech-Rodriguez (2002) observe that the most predominant change in the composition of the Latino family consists of more unmarried Latinas in the population or single heads of household who have younger children at younger ages outside of wedlock.

Two of the most predominant reasons that are affecting change within the Latino/a family are economics and immigration issues (Vega 1995). For many years economics has been the authoritative issue in the composition of the Latino/a families. Migration has proved to be a good source of income for entire families for years and continues to appear strong in spite of the most competent workforce. There are differences, though, as migration has become less and less a family event. In years past, migration would include every member of the family and some neighbors, distant relatives, and friends. Nowadays, fewer families do this (losing the sense of community), the young adults refuse to go and prefer to work locally (dismembering the family), and friends and distant relatives are ever more difficult to bring along. Fathers away from home are one more of the strains that the quest for economic survival exerts on the Latino/a family. Many Latino fathers work in terrestrial transportation, that is, trucking, thereby having to be absent from home for long periods of time (one to two weeks). Those who do not travel are forced to work long hours to add some overtime to their gaunt paychecks. Finally, women and men are being equally forced to work at the same time. Long forgotten is the wife who stays home and takes care of the children, at least among less prosperous Latino/as (who are the majority). This is not necessarily a bad thing, since it invests Latina women with decision-making power, equality of rights, and options in unfavorable times. These factors all contribute to the new appearance of the Latino/a family.

Immigration issues are the second constituent of this dyad of affairs changing the composition of our families. Much of our Latino/a population (legal and illegal) consists of individuals who have been separated from their families and their communities. Looking for new opportunities, many persons like us have immigrated at the expense of leaving behind many loved ones. For the most fortunate of us, this is simply a temporary measure, but for many others, it is a long and costly process that takes a huge toll in the sound thread of the family's internal composition. It can also add to the already-recognized resilience of our Latino/a people, who in the midst of much adversity seem to get closer and stronger.

The pastoral counselor then needs to consider the metamorphic changes of the Latino/a family and design intervening strategies appropriate to the new reality of our most established institution. This need invites us to introduce feminist therapy as a model to consider when working with Latino/a families. Feminist therapy began to be a serious actor in the field of psychotherapy in the 1970s. Under its principles, feminist therapy challenges the expectation for consultees to adapt to traditional family roles. It also confronts the cultural principle of using maleness as a standard of normality. Finally, it rejects the idea of biological determinism so prevalent within Latino/a circles (Bertrando and Toffanetti 2004). Family therapy then is a good option when the pastoral counselor is committed to supporting the healing process of our historically oppressed women.

TRADITIONAL ROLES WITHIN LATINO/A FAMILIES

Even though this shifting of the Latino/a family has greatly affected the role assumption of family members, traditional roles continue to depict a standard to pursue in our Latino/a communities. As Aída Hurtado (1995, 45) writes, in spite of the increased participation of working wives in family decisions, working and nonworking wives "both agreed authority should rest in the husband/father regardless of wife's employment status." This view becomes a solid point of departure when establishing communication with the family.

The authority role of wives is a silent part, valued for its ability to retain control while giving husbands/fathers the contrary impression. In other words, Latina women remain in control while traditional family roles, including the husband/father as head of household, remain undisturbed.

Derald Wing Sue and David Sue (2003) mention some of the most traditional roles of Latino/a families. Grandparents represent wisdom, mothers abnegation, fathers responsibility, children obedience, and godparents resourcefulness. The faithful fulfillment of family roles assures the integrity of the family. This is also a frequent field of dispute among family members because of the recurrent breaks of their expectations concerning role boundaries that are normal in their family interactions. This is then one of the places where the counselor may need to render full attention while trying to identify possible stressors in the functioning of the family.

If we consider that the traditional role assumption within Latino/a families is prevalent, we need to consider that husbands and parents are going to be more prone to resist therapy and deny their expression of feelings. The traditional husband role entails that he be strong enough to protect and provide for the family, as well as hardworking, responsible, and therefore the dispenser of stability at home. This role seems difficult to reconcile with the open expression of feelings and open discussion of personal issues that are expected in therapy. With this in mind, the pastoral counselor will want to give all family members explicit permission to express feelings openly (Goldenberg and Goldenberg 2002).

When the therapist meets the Rodriguez family, he is going to notice how Linda allows Tomas to take the initiative in the conversation but at the same time is prompt to fill in the gaps and add remarks to Tomas's discourse, showing an implicit authoritative role within the family. While discussing spiritual matters, Linda will immediately take the initiative and talk passionately about their confidence in God and their decision to leave God in charge. Teresa will occupy the role of the oldest child, since her brother Jorge Alberto is not present, and she probably will be physically closer to Linda than to Tomas. Junior will probably be either closer to his father or significantly isolated from the rest of the family members. Other relatives and/or friends present might choose to remain silent, leave the room, or stand up during the consultation. They may stand up when the counselor arrives and remain standing, or may sit periodically. All this behavior describes the traditional roles of Latino/a families, so it might be consistent with the reality of the Rodriguez family. Variations of this picture are countless and must be expected. Nonetheless, the pastoral counselor has a clear picture that serves as a point of reference in becoming adept at identifying deviations to the rule. This represents Robert L. Smith and Patricia Stevens-Smith's (1992) idea of the therapist emphasizing the healthy functioning of the family as a premise to use in determining a course of interaction.

NEGOTIATING CULTURAL IDENTITY

Maria T. Flores (2000) speaks of the increasing clashes common to Latino/a families as they are forced to negotiate their cultural identity. Most Latino/a families in the United States are here as the result of a family member immigrating at some point in the family's historical account. Many families are therefore composed of immigrant members (mostly parents) plus members who were born or raised in the States (mostly children) and, therefore, are heavily influenced by the cultural values of U.S. society. Thus, two different cultural preferences reside within the same house. These two different cultural preferences bring together two different sets of negotiating techniques, two different sets of preferred communication, two different sets of scripts for showing and attaining intimacy, two different sets of values and mores, and two different sets of preferred disciplinary rules.

This problem is easily appreciated in the language preference of family members (Goldenberg and Goldenberg 2002). Older adults will most probably prefer to speak in their original language, while younger family members will favor the use of English as the functioning language at home and with the community at large. We differentiate "functioning language" and "language of the heart," which remains the language of choice to communicate heart matters, including prayer. Goldenberg and Goldenberg (2002) also mention the encounter of collectivism and individualism in these families as a point of conflict. This can be related to changing cultural identity and the changes that occur in attitudes concerning collectivism and individualism within the family. The pastoral counselor's responsibility to avoid rushing to label withdrawn members of the family as being isolated, especially younger members, is especially important.

With this in mind, the pastoral counselor will be able to address Teresa and Junior in English. He will be willing to compromise his own conversational style to meet the one used by the younger members of the Rodriguez family (mimicking). He will expect discourse from these younger members to be more to the point, factual, and rationalized. He will address them directly and avoid letting them mediate the family discourse. Finally, the pastoral counselor will be willing to mediate between both parents and children when these differences appear to be hindering the healthy processing of the particular distressful event.

If the issue seems to be precisely this negotiating of cultural identity, Flores (2000) recommends the use of narrative therapy techniques that allow the family to visualize, discuss, and renegotiate their stand. Songs, poems, histories, and letters are all beneficial tools that are easy to use with distinctive individuals of a family because they serve the purpose of imprinting value on each one of the generations. Narrative tools are also important to therapy because they can be used as practical tasks that can be carried out at home, extending the reach of the therapeutic encounter beyond the limits of the visit. They could also be instrumental as a preparation for therapy, as in the use of the intake questionnaire. The intake questionnaire is also a fundamental tool that allows the counselor to gather demographic information that is important to consider and would result in a nuisance if gathered within the context of the initial interview.

STRUCTURAL FAMILY THERAPY

Salvador Minuchin's amazing work in *Tecnicas de terapia familiar* (1984/2004) and *Families and Family Therapy* (1974) is behind many of the therapeutic tools we have considered in this chapter. Minuchin is considered the main figure of the structural model for family therapy (Hanna and Brown 1999; Gladding 2002). This model of family therapy regards the family's organizational structure as the grantor of family stability (homeostasis) or family disturbance. Identified problems are but symptoms of more elaborate issues pertaining, for the most part, to the same organizational structure and the crossing of boundaries within subsystems.

In this model, the family therapist closely observes communication patterns among family members and uses those observations to formulate hypotheses that, after being tested within the therapeutic encounter, will lead the therapist to choose the appropriate intervention to help the family. The goal of this model is to destabilize the ill family structure by a process of therapeutic alliances that will help the family to strengthen system and subsystem boundaries, which are the most frequent cause of family problems.

This succinct summary does not do justice to the richness of the concepts that are part of this model. Nevertheless, we want to recognize the effort of this Latino physician who is considered one of the giants of family therapy. We invite the pastoral counselor to become familiar, through further investigation, with these and other theories that will facilitate the flexibility required while counseling families, especially Latino/a families, who in their diversity represent an even bigger challenge to the capacity of the helper.

10

PASTORAL STRATEGIES FOR ISSUES OF DISCRIMINATION AND RACISM

We have experienced racism in our native countries (Venezuela and Colombia) but became keenly aware of this social plague toward the end of the first year of our experience in the United States. In our countries, the mestizo population is the largest, but the power and leadership are held by white-skinned people. The outer reality of the bigger cities was not much different from the microcosm we had experienced growing up.

THE NATURE OF RACISM

When we talk about the nature of racism, we refer to the factors, conditions, and ideas that are behind the racist and discriminatory attitude of some people (usually the dominant group) against a different other (usually those at the margins). Alexander Thomas and Samuel Sillen (1972) are quick to identify two of the dominant themes that have been a landmark in the history of racist America, themes that—despite our apparent progress in social matters—continue to offer a significant challenge to every effort in support of more egalitarian conditions for our society. These two themes are, first, the idea that Blacks are biologically (genetically) inferior to whites, especially in regard to their mental and reasoning capacities, and second, the idea that Blacks are more prone, by either "nature" or "nurture," to personality pathology.

Before we discuss the implications of these two themes in the social practice of our society, as well as their impact on our Latino/a population, we need to consider a subtler but essential issue. This problem is usually addressed as the "sociological construction of race" (Rothenberg 2001). This term implies that the modern reflection on race is a mere sociological construction without biological basis. In other words, we have come to realize that talking about a pure, genetically isolated group such as "Black" or "white" is nearly impossible, due to the social dynamics of our modern world (immigration, globalization, colonization, etc.). This is a clear dynamic that, nevertheless, has not stopped us from making categorizations and distinctions based on skin color, hair type, facial features, and other physical characteristics. Here we tend to agree with Thomas C. Holt (2000), who cleverly has pointed out how this "social construction" of race is a social construct without impact beyond academia.

Thus, even though scientific research has proved there is no such a thing as a pure race, we need to consider the social reality of "race" as the principle behind racism. We need to consider that we continue to make distinctions based on differences (mostly physical differences) among groups (Marger 1994). In other words, if we recall Thomas and Sillen's (1972) themes of racism, we know that at some point we will fall into the category of either "Black" or "white." It certainly seems arbitrary to pull people out of the diverse social pool to fit them into either of these two groups. But it is precisely this arbitrary social practice that originates the racial and social discriminatory dynamic that makes Latino/as a socially oppressed group in American society.

Even though some authors, including Martin N. Marger (1994), tend to identify three major categories (Caucasoid, Mongoloid, and Negroid), we have chosen to follow the more classical interpretation of race as a basic "Black" and "white" dilemma (Schaefer 2000; Cox 2000). As mentioned, this grouping is certainly arbitrary but serves the purpose of clearly contrasting the dominant group and those at the margins, which is basically the dynamic that feeds the inhumane reality of racism. Under these conditions, it appears clear that racism is possible only from the dominant group down. Talking about racism from the oppressed group upward is just one more of the fallacies elaborated to masquerade this unjust practice. As stated by Richard T. Schaefer (2000, 15), "Racism is a doctrine of racial supremacy."

This statement introduces us to a point that is important for differentiating the common actions of groups at the margins (including Latino/as) that are wrongly labeled "racism." Here we are referring to prejudice. This is a delicate theme, since we are mostly familiar with the negative associations that the word *prejudice* brings to mind. What we have failed to recognize is the positive component that forms part of prejudice. This positive component makes prejudice a survival tool necessary for groups at the margins. James M. Jones (1997, 10) defines prejudice as "a positive or negative attitude, judgment, or feeling about a person that is generalized from attitudes or beliefs held about the group to which the person belongs."

Prejudice clearly appears as a racist element that leads us to favor those of the similar group while demeaning the different. Nonetheless, the operational pattern of this element is quite distinct for the dominant and the oppressed group. For the oppressed, prejudice means alertness against the system and against practices that suppress them and deprive them of the opportunities needed to make an impact in their lives and in the life of the group. In contrast, prejudice of the dominant group is an excluding practice that diminishes the value and the capacities of the oppressed.

This behavioral practice of prejudice gives shape to the final element of racism: "discrimination" (Jones 1997). Discrimination is prejudice acted upon, by either individual or institutional means, against a different group. Favoring means neglecting, and in this case, this practice appears to be colorless because both groups tend to disregard cultural differences in favor of their own kind. Discrimination is highly associated with institutional policies and system processes in which one group uses profiling as a selection mechanism. Discriminatory practices usually go beyond phenotypes to include elements as varied as political affiliation, cultural background, and sexual orientation.

TYPES OF RACISM

Jones (1997) identifies three different types of racism: individual, institutional, and cultural. Individual racism, which is the "closest to race prejudice" (p. 13), is characterized by the belief that one's race is superior to another. This is merely an internal process, and even though the person may act on this prejudice, the real problem is posed by the thinking process that places others as inferior just based on their racial characteristics. Meanwhile, institutional racism is the use of duly erected institutions as an instrument to act out individual racism. Lawrence Blum (2002) gives an interesting example of this type of racism when he mentions seniority as a perpetuating mechanism of the unequal employment opportunities of earlier years in America. By mentioning this example, Blum cleverly identifies how deeply institutional racism is carved into the fabric of our society. Although we agree with Blum in recognizing the practical principles behind seniority, it is fascinating to think about the role that race has played in shaping our living structures.

Finally, we encounter cultural racism, which is described by Jones (1997) as both individual and institutional beliefs of superiority based on race and/or cultural heritage. Cultural racism is highly significant in today's reality, since it has become the predominant form used by the dominant group either to isolate or assimilate the groups at the margins. Cultural racism is certainly not as blunt as biological racism, but it has the same implications and the same roots. One group (culture) is superior, and the other is inferior, in need of redemption (becoming assimilated), or doomed to its inferior place in cases where assimilation is not a viable option. Holt (2000, 14), quoting Étienne Balibar, lets us perceive the extent that cultural racism has reached in our modern society: "There is, he observed, a 'new racism' abroad, 'a racism without races,' in which culture takes on the function previously fulfilled by biology." This type of racism is aggressive and deceptive, since it usually bears the facade of civilization and modernism, but it is only continuing with the racist dynamics that have been long since condemned.

We could certainly say that cultural racism is a mutation of biological racism that, in its pursuit to prevail in a changing world, has adapted to the same conditions that at one point threatened its existence. Here we refer to some of the characteristic elements of our modern world, including colonization, immigration, intermarriage, and a number of other conditions that have made biological race a thing of the past. To its discredit, cultural racism has become an even more fearsome enemy, since it disguises itself under subtler terms and then uses more socially acceptable weapons such as assimilation. Nonetheless, it is racism to the core.

ELEMENTS OF INTERNALIZED OPPRESSION

It is part of our human nature to look for the fault in others without first observing our own fault. The Christian tradition warns us against looking at the speck in our brother's or sister's eye while disregarding the log that is in ours (Matthew 7:3). The attitude of concentrating on what is lacking in others and seeing others as "less than" can be found in many religious writings. For instance, a cursory reading of the Hebrew Bible indicates that a particular group of people might be superior based on their faith. This illusion of superiority has fostered xenophobia, justified oppression, and promoted genocide among different religious groups to this day. The oppressive attitude prevailing among the powers that be is also seen in their action and conduct toward the marginalized, such as women, children, and the physically ill or disabled.

A. K. Wesley (2002) addresses the genealogies of Genesis 10 and 1 Chronicles 1:1—2:55 as examples of this tendency of the people of Israel to show discriminatory attitudes against other peoples not belonging to the promise. This attitude ascribes an inferiority label to all those who do not belong, an attitude that is clearly seen in Christian tradition when in Jesus' discourse they are paralleled with "dogs" (Matthew 15:26). But it is the discriminatory attitude within the chosen people that concerns us at this point, since it is a reflection of what we commonly overlook within our Latino/a communities when discussing racism and discrimination. In other words, we readily see the racially discriminatory attitudes of others toward us, but we are not so quick to see our discriminatory attitudes toward those like us, those within the group.

When reading passages of the Christian and Hebrew tradition that discount women and children (Exodus 12:37; Joshua 8:35; Matthew 14:21; 15:38; Acts 4:4), what we are actually reading is the oppressive yoke that their same people put upon them. In these cases, failure to count women and children is indicative of their unvalued status. For pastoral counselors working with Latino/a communities, this is a priority in our own struggle against racism and discrimination. Several "isms" are entrenched within us and demean our efforts to do justice to those who historically have been neglected and overpowered within the limits of our own communities. It is true that we need to raise our voices against the racial conditions that keep us at the margins, but we first need to speak aloud against internalized oppression.

Sexism

Paula S. Rothenberg (2001, 97) defines sexism as "the oppression of women by men in a society that is largely patriarchal." Although this is certainly the bottom line, sexism is a more intricate reality that is characterized in great part by role assumption and "intergroup" perceptions (Eckes, Trautner, and Behrendt 2005). Basing their observations on Tajfel's social identity theory, Thomas Eckes, Hanns M. Trautner, and Regina Behrendt were able to reflect on the early favoritism of children's choices related to belonging to their respective gender group. As soon as children have consciousness of their gender (at five to seven years of age), they begin to favor those belonging to their group (male or female). Even more interesting, this initial childhood "hostility" toward the other gender group transforms in adolescence into a protective and patronizing attitude, at least from boys toward girls (Eckes, Trautner, and Behrendt 2005). This dynamic is usually associated with the pressure that society exerts on fulfilling gender roles such as "protector," "provider," and "tough" for males, and "homemaker," "passive," and "weak" for females, which in turn constitutes the second element that defines sexism (Rothenberg 1988).

Even though this particular dynamic is not unique for Latino/as, it certainly has a great influence in our communities, where we continue subjugating women and relegating them to roles traditionally associated with femaleness. This is certainly another form of oppression that is clearly observable at home, where still many Latino men feel reluctant to help with domestic tasks such as cleaning, cooking, and doing laundry. One would think that this reality is certainly changing in a society that demands both partners as part of the labor force, but the truth is that in our role as pastoral counselors, we witness many examples in which hardworking Latina women are solely responsible for homemaking tasks regardless of their bread earner status. This is but one of the several examples we could name as a part of the sexist mentality that represents a stumbling block to any effort of making Latino/a communities a cohesive entity willing to stand on its own.

Machismo

This theme of sexism within the Latino/a culture is strongly associated with the theme of machismo. The term *machismo* is certainly controversial and is commonly avoided in modern discourse because of its negative associations with the drunkard-abusive male, which adds to the poor image of Latinos (Anaya 1996; Mirandé 1997). Nonetheless, a different reading of machismo parallels with the role assumptions that continue costing so much of the emotional well-being of our Latino/a communities. In this sense, machismo connotes the emotionally unavailable male who sees the expression of feelings as weakness and therefore improper for a real man. "Men don't cry," we are taught from childhood, reinforcing the wrongful notion of toughness and stiffness as part of what being a man means. This attitude is without doubt at the root of many family problems for our Latino/a men and women, especially when we consider that emotionally unavailable men mean emotionally unavailable husbands and emotionally unavailable fathers. Machismo, thus seen, constitutes a workable element within the setting of pastoral counseling, and one that requires much attention and effort from us.

Nativism

The term *nativism* reflects the anti-immigrant exclusionary sentiment that has populated American society during diverse instances of modern history (Delgado and Stefancic 1998; Kilty and De Haymes 2000). This sentiment is not in any way exclusively linked to Latino/a immigration. Almost every immigrant community in the States has, at one point or another, dealt with this hostile attitude. Nonetheless, we could certainly say that, during the last decade, Latino/as immigrating to the United States have been at the focal point of this anti-immigrant theme. Several factors contribute to this, but at a glance, we can point to the high immigration rate of Latino/as and the rapid growth of our population as the predominant elements that contribute to this widespread posture in American society.

Since we are focusing on the internalized oppression that is at the root of many of our problems as a Latino/a community, we need to address the troublesome reality of nativism among our own Latino/a people. This sentiment is usually found among American-born Latino/as and already-established immigrants who look with suspicion upon those of us who are just arriving. This is brought about in a spirit of competition and jealousy that sees other Latino/as as a threat instead of as possible allies against the racism and discrimination we face in this society at large. It is a sad situation that is corroding our innermost fiber and poses a particular challenge to pastoral counselors because of its silent and insidious nature.

Classism

It is important for us to add to the discussion a final element that contributes greatly to the internalized oppression of our Latino/a people. Classism is an imported concept that we have brought out of our highly stratified Latino societies and applied in the United States to discriminate against our own. Classism is then a foreign element misplaced in a society with a well-organized and established middle class. This middle class breaches the abysmal difference of opportunities and available resources that exists between rich and poor, and at the same time makes it more difficult to exclude others based on their economic and social status.

If in one of our Latino/a countries, having a car and house represents stability, in the United States it is just a necessity, and one that is reached by a great majority regardless of their economic position. Some of us nonetheless continue under the illusion of our financial prosperity as a segregating mechanism whereby we fill a need to set ourselves apart from the rest. Under this illusion, we then categorize, judge, and most of the time exclude others on the basis of their acquisition power. By doing this, we fragment the Latino/a body even more, and again we do it from within.

Racial and cultural neocolonialism

For the most part, we are quite familiar with the concept of colonialism in which a given country extends its sovereignty over another country or territory beyond the country's marked boundaries. Because of the many times and aggressive means (military and political) by which this happens, this practice is almost nonexistent in our modern society. Unfortunately, however, neocolonialism has emerged as a new practice in which the "colonization" process occurs mainly on an economical level. The influence and economic impact of developed countries over our poor nations is of such a magnitude that most of our sovereign policies are directly linked to practices that favor economic and ideological exchange as established by this handful of wealthy countries.

This "domination" has extended, as anyone would expect, beyond the political and economic arenas. Racial and cultural neocolonialism is the new trend of our times. By means of this new form of colonialism, less powerful nations are being misled into the idea that their culture and phenotypes are of less quality, inferior

to those of their rich and powerful neighbors. In this "westerniza-
tion process" (Feagin and Feagin 1999), the West (Euro-American
countries) is portrayed as civilized, cultured, refined, decent, and
beautiful, while the rest of us are portrayed as uncivil, uneducated,
vulgar, dishonest, and not as good-looking.

   This, of course, is not new. Beginning with religion and its
white, blue-eyed images of saints, to Hollywood and the blond
superheroes, we encounter day after day numerous messages that
consciously or unconsciously continue adding to the self-image
of our Latino/a people. This is probably the force behind a grandmother's decision to ask her daughter to look intently at a blue-
eyed doll while pregnant with the hope of changing the baby's eyes
to blue in utero. This same idea was behind the grandmother's
daily practice of rubbing white powder on her granddaughter's
black skin in order to whiten it a little more. Behind these examples clearly appears the true nature of racial and cultural neocolonialism when it convinces us that black is ugly, that our tinted skin
is proof of our inferior nature.

   It is precisely here where this process has its pinnacle, when
we Latino/as, as colonized people, accept our inferiority status
based on racial and cultural stereotypes (Feagin and Feagin 1999;
Freire 2000). We constantly do this when we allow ourselves to feel
ashamed of our language, origin, feasts, color, and traditions. But
most importantly, we perpetuate this rationale of the dominant
group when we fail to see the beauty that is in us as a people. We
are a beautiful and bountiful mix of peoples, cultures, colors, and
languages. We need to feel proud of our origins and our traditions. We need to feel proud of our struggles and the resilience of
our heritage. We cannot forget what we are, because what we are
is beautiful in extreme measure. After the grandma's attempts to
whiten her granddaughter had failed, the child's mother decided
to make her feel as pretty and beautiful as she was, and she did it
by teaching her this little verse:

> *Morenita soy señores, yo no niego mi color.*
> [Sirs, I am Brown skinned, and I do not deny my color.]
> *Y entre rosas y azucenas lo Moreno es lo mejor.*
> [And among roses and lilies, the brown is the best.]

This is precisely what we do as pastoral counselors working with Latino/as; we assure them of their value, their capacities, and their resources. We remind them and ourselves of the richness of our varied cultures and peoples. We encourage the use of native languages and the preservation of the same as an invaluable tool. We celebrate our Latino/a traditions and feasts. We remember and honor our forebearers and our heroes. We present new role models of Latino/as who make a difference in their families, communities, nations, and the world. We speak loudly of our Latino/a pride and encourage others to do the same. Then we can say that among roses and lilies, the Latino/a is what is best.

THE PROBLEM OF ASSIMILATION

As stated by Melissa Michelson (2003), assimilation is part of the process of cultural learning into which an immigrant enters when in contact with a new culture. This process of "cultural learning" is usually known as acculturation, and acculturation can happen as assimilation or as separation. Acculturation as assimilation is characterized by the rejection of one's own culture in order to adopt the new culture. Acculturation as separation maintains the group's own values and cultural baggage while resisting the process of neglect and finally forgetfulness that is prevalent in assimilation.

This process of assimilation is closely linked to the idea of racial and cultural neocolonialism. Only when individuals are willing to accept their own culture as inferior and unworthy will they be willing to sacrifice what stands at the core of their being. We are willing to trade what we are because we see a probable gain in doing so. For instance, in a bilingual home, we choose to speak only English because it will make attending school easier for our children. The family obtains the expected result by paying a high price of not considering the advantages of being bilingual individuals.

This cultural trading is commonly done out of shame and embarrassment. Assimilation is certainly a cruel path for us Latino/as seeking to make America our new homeland. It is a violent process that deprives us of what constitutes our beauty and our richness. In this sense, we agree with Michelson (2003), who has signaled the process of separation or, as she prefers to call it, the "ethnic competition theory" as the proper path of acculturation for Latino/as. Thus, we retain our values, beliefs, customs, traditions, languages, and so on, while at the same time learning from the new culture. In summary, this ethnic competition theory tells us that we do not need to lose what we are in order to acculturate; we can achieve success in this society without Americanizing our last names; we can be productive and good citizens without trading Cinco de Mayo for Fourth of July; we can be beautiful without blond hair and blue eyes. Assimilation is not the only way to acculturation. We have a choice. The choice is to believe in ourselves as a people.

COMPETENCES OF MULTICULTURAL PASTORAL COUNSELORS

A theory known as Multicultural Counseling Competencies, or MCC (Santiago-Rivera, Arredondo, and Gallardo-Cooper 2002), has become a common point of reference for diversity competence. These authors mention three multicultural competencies that are usually identified as fundamental in working with diverse populations: awareness, knowledge, and skills (Smith et al. 2004). Moreover, we want to include one more multicultural competency that we consider of great importance when working with Latino/as: cultural empathy (Ridley and Udipi 2002).

Awareness is a term we have used on multiple occasions in this book, and we consider it a fundamental trait of any pastoral counselor. As a multicultural competency, awareness means, among other things, to know our own prejudices and biases, to be conscious of our cultural stereotypes and assumptions, to understand our theoretical orientations and their possible limitations while working with Latino/as, and to recognize our own style of communication and how it influences our effectiveness as counselors (Smith et al. 2004). This process of awareness is constant and broad, reaching beyond the therapeutic setting and serving as a check-and-balance tool for the therapist's effectiveness.

But the pastoral counselor not only knows him- or herself, he or she also knows about the culture of the individuals who form part of the counselor's practice. Thus, our pastoral counselor is aware of the multiplicity of racial categories, nationalities, languages, and traditions of the Latino/a culture (Casas, Vasquez, and

Ruiz de Esparza 2002). J. Manuel Casas, Melba J. T. Vasquez, and Christopher A. Ruiz de Esparza also remind us that it is important to be aware of demographics such as family composition within Latino/a communities, as well as sociohistorical elements such as the length of time since immigration. In addition, it is also important to consider the socioeconomic status, including the individual's level of education and the "acculturation stressors" the particular individual might be facing (Arredondo and Pérez 2003). Even though our hope with this book is to facilitate learning for every pastoral counselor, we know that we are far from reaching a thorough knowledge of all these variants. In such a case, genuineness is regarded as the path to follow (Smith et al. 2004). Pretending to know is a significant hindrance in our efforts to establish a sincere relationship with the consultee. It is always better to recognize our ignorance and invite our consultee to enrich our knowledge of his or her culture.

We mentioned skills as a third multicultural competency within the therapeutic setting. Here we are referring to the actual ability of the pastoral counselor to use interventions appropriate to the culture of the consultee. This implies that the therapist has the capacity and flexibility to move back and forth between different theoretical models and practical approaches to therapy. If we consider the diversity within the Latino/a culture, we know that this is a challenge, especially to the pastoral counselor who has decided to become comfortable with a handful of strategies and interventions set beforehand.

Finally, we have encountered cultural empathy, which as defined by Charles R. Ridley and Sharranya Udipi (2002, 318), is the "ability of counselors to understand accurately the self-experiences of clients from different cultures." In other words, the pastoral counselor needs to understand that each individual represents a set of diverse and unique cultural interactions that give shape to his or her self-experiences. This approach entails a profound respect for the consultee's traditions, spiritual pilgrimage, and culturally learned behaviors and expressions. Likewise, it becomes an invitation to develop a working alliance between both parties in which the therapist feels encouraged to ask for clarification and explanation of unknown particulars of the culture.

TOWARD A HEALTHY PARANOIA

Daisuke Akiba and Cynthia García Coll (2004) comment on what has usually been called healthy cultural paranoia, which is the mechanism used by minorities and oppressed groups to maintain a state of alertness against the rather common unjust participatory rules of our societies. This cultural paranoia is seen in the African American grandmother who prepares her grandchildren to face extra hardships and tighter scrutiny against them than against children of the dominant group. Thus, healthy cultural paranoia is awareness of the advantages and disadvantages of the system and applies to the positioning of the group within the same.

In spite of the struggles that we face because of our Latino/a identity, we as a people have been slow to recognize the unjust circumstances that hold us tight in the oppressive yoke of the dominant group. Moreover, on many occasions, we have also fallen into denial of these oppressive circumstances or have simply gotten comfortable with them. This all adds up to even greater vulnerability to racism and discrimination, and by the same token, it makes our children and grandchildren more vulnerable to the same conditions that we have endured.

The healthy paranoia encouraged by the African American grandma is good to imitate, because our African American brothers and sisters have gotten adept at using this tool to their advantage. It has benefited them in surviving in a society where they are sometimes not welcome, and it could be beneficial for Latino/as to use their model. Our children could learn that being Latino/a is not a given and that there is much work ahead of us if we ever dream of changing the conditions that have shrunk our horizons. Our children would learn to recognize the subtleties that make a difference when we want to be treated with equality. Finally, our children will learn that they need to be active participants in this struggle by fighting these same discriminatory practices within the realm of our own group. By embracing this healthy paranoia, making good use of their creativity and resiliency, and celebrating their self-efficacy, Latino/as will then continue to move toward a better life in relationship to self, family, and culture.

Closing Remarks

LISTENING—CHOOSING THE BEST PART

Pastoral counseling is about listening to people's thoughts, emotions, behaviors, and patterns of relationships. It is about listening to their "innermost," their souls. Pastoral counselors as God's representatives commit themselves to providing a milieu where people can have a voice, power, and a healing connection. This goes in accord with the fact of having been created in God's image.

The Lord has a voice: "The voice of the Lord is powerful; the voice of the Lord is majestic. The voice of the Lord breaks the cedars. . . . The voice of the Lord strikes with flashes of lightning. The voice of the Lord shakes the desert; the Lord shakes the Desert of Kadesh" (Psalm 29:4-8, NIV). Pastoral counselors give Latino/as a voice when they listen to their concerns without judging or condemning them. They listen when they suspend their personal needs and avoid imposing their individualistic views. Pastoral counselors give Hispanics a voice when they overcome the temptation to prescribe simplistic solutions to socially ingrained issues. They give them a voice when they encourage Hispanics to question oppressive systems and to question the Lord's actions.

Darrell J. Fasching and Dell Dechant (2001) suggest that in the story found in the book of Job, the one who is on trial is God. Job is questioning God's justice, God's behavior, and God's goodness. Job is protesting God's silence and unjust treatment. He initiated his faithful protest by cursing the day of his birth and saying, "May the day of my birth perish, and the night it was said, 'A boy is born'" (Job 3:1-3 NIV). He continues listing the number of complaints to include his perception on how unjust the Lord was being with him, to the point of calling God a tyrant (6:24, 29; 7:20; 9:2, 16-17; 9:32-35). The friends who come to "comfort" Job appoint themselves as God's defense lawyers. Job later calls them "worthless" and quack healers:

"You, however, smear me with lies; you are worthless physicians, all of you! If only you would be altogether silent! For you, that would be wisdom. Hear now my argument; listen to the plea of my lips. Will you speak wickedly on God's behalf? Will you speak deceitfully for him? Will you show him partiality? Will you argue the case for God?" (Job 13:4-8, NIV)

The story ends with God firing the self-appointed attorneys and agreeing with Job (Job 42:7-11). Job is assured that his suffering was unjust and undeserved but that he was not alone. God actually was suffering along with him.

This reading confirms God's commitment to give people a voice, even a voice to protest the Lord's actions. Pastoral counselors give a voice to Hispanics when they are allowed to quarrel with God: "Why are you doing this to me?" "Don't you think I have suffered enough?" "My faithfulness is in vain!" "How is it that you don't care and abandon us?" Justo L. González (1990) and Ismael Garcia (1997) point out that the issue for most Latino/as is not the existence of God, but rather wondering about the actions they attribute to God: "Where were you when my little one was shot?"

The pastoral counselor empowers Latino/as when he or she concentrates on their strengths, resilience, and their own resources to face their emotional, relational, or mental challenges. God is powerful and gives strength to his people (Psalm 68:35). The pastoral counselor empowers Hispanics when he or she recognizes and celebrates their conquering spirit. The pastoral counselor establishes a healing connection with Latino/as when he or she listens, accepts, embraces, respects, and cares for them.

This kind of accurate and empathetic listening attitude is illustrated in the ministry provided by Mary, Martha's sister, who chose listening as the best way to help a person in crisis:

As Jesus and his disciples were on their way, he came to a village where a woman named Martha opened her home to him. She had a sister called Mary, who sat at the Lord's feet listening to what he said. But Martha was distracted by all the preparations that had to be made. She came to him and asked, "Lord, don't you care that my sister has left me to do the work by myself? Tell her to help me!" "Martha, Martha," the Lord answered, "You are worried and upset about many things, but only one thing is needed. Mary has chosen what is better, and it will not be taken away from her." (Luke 10:38-42, NIV)

Mary sat, indicating that she put herself at the same level and made an intentional choice to listen to her friend, Jesus of Nazareth. Jesus was on his way to Jerusalem, and his ministry was approaching the end (Luke 9:51). He came to perhaps the only place where he felt safe and did not need to be protecting himself from those who were seeking an opportunity to eliminate him (Wuellner and Leslie 1984). Mary, with great attending skills, offered him an inviting atmosphere in which he could explore his emotions and feelings.

We do not have the verbatim transcript for this encounter, but it could easily be recreated. Jesus has invested his time, financial resources, and talents in helping his disciples understand the principles of his reign. After almost three years, it seems that the disciples have not understood or embraced his ideas and project. This might have been intensely disappointing to Jesus, and perhaps this was part of his sharing with Mary, along with his feelings of frustration, depression, and anger with himself for not having advanced his mission as he had anticipated. The canonical Gospels reveal that his sense of failure and depression were leading him to question whether the plan was worthy. He even felt abandoned by his Father. Mary is attentively listening to him, responding with care, genuinely engaged, and with an empathetic heart. She is present and *disponible* (Marcel 1950), meaning that she is willing to dispose herself to allow Jesus to feel at home. Perhaps Martha, as she is listening to this deep sharing and Jesus' tears, has become anxious and decides to interrupt the process by suggesting to Mary that she move from being to doing. Jesus tells Martha that Mary has chosen the best: to listen to a human being in crisis. The idea is for pastoral counselors to follow the lead of Mary. Isn't it interesting that it was a marginalized, despised, and oppressed person, a woman, who took the time to listen to the Lord and Savior in his time of crisis?

Pastoral counselors connect with Latino/as when they appreciate the diversity among them and embrace their multicultural-mosaic nature. There is unity in the sense of purpose, suffering, and hope, but the diversity is so vast that trying to put Latino/as into one category is delusional. Ellen Van Wolde (1997) offers a peripheral reading of what is traditionally called the tower of Babel, but she prefers to call it "The Story of the Dispersion of the Human Beings." She suggests that the main point of the story is to present the diversity of languages as a condition for the dispersion and happiness of human beings. God's strategy to disperse human beings was to eliminate homogeneity, discourage uniformity, and create many different languages.

Fasching and Dechant (2001) submit that the story of Babel is a call to move from ethnocentrism to interdependence. They believe that uniformity of languages, ideas, beliefs, and values is the perfect "agar" or gel culture for growing religious prejudice and all kinds of isms, such as sexism and racism.

> The Lord said, "If as one people speaking the same language they have begun to do this, then nothing they plan to do will be impossible for them. Come, let us go down and confuse their language so they will not understand each other." So the Lord scattered them from there over all the earth, and they stopped building the city. That is why it was called Babel—because there the Lord confused the language of the whole world. From there the Lord scattered them over the face of the whole earth. (Genesis 11:6-9, NIV)

According to Fasching and Dechant (2001, 299), "God saw that human efforts to reach the holy were misguided and so reoriented human efforts by creating a world of strangers where the holy is to be encountered in the midst of diversity—through the encounter with the stranger."

Competent multicultural pastoral counselors understand that we find God amidst diversity and therefore use prophetic authority and power to denounce attempts to silence and isolate Latino/as. As God's ambassadors, they have the same "agenda," which is to promote justice, to embrace grace, and to walk in humbleness. "This is what the Lord Almighty says: 'Administer true justice; show mercy and compassion to one another. Do not oppress the widow or the fatherless, the alien or the poor. In your hearts do not think evil of each other'" (Zechariah 7:9-10 NIV). *Paz.*

BIBLIOGRAPHY

Akiba, D., and C. G. Coll (2004). "Effective Interventions with Children of Color and Their Families: A Contextual Developmental Approach." In *Practicing Multiculturalism: Affirming Diversity in Counseling and Psychology*, ed. T. B. Smith, 123–44. Boston: Pearson.

Anaya, R. (1996). "'I'm the King': The Macho Image." In Muy macho: *Latino Men Confront Their Manhood*, ed. R. Gonzalez, 57–73. New York: Doubleday.

Angelou, M. (1994). *On the Pulse of Morning.* New York: Random House.

Arredondo, P., and P. Pérez (2003). "Counseling Paradigms and Latina/o Americans: Contemporary Considerations." In *Culture and Counseling: New Approaches*, ed. F. Harper and J. McFadden, 115–32. Boston: Pearson Education.

Bagarozzi, D. A. (2001). *Enhancing Intimacy in Marriage: A Clinician's Guide.* New York: Brunner-Routledge.

Bakan, D. (1968). *Disease, Pain, and Sacrifice: Toward a Psychology of Suffering.* Chicago: University of Chicago Press.

Baumgartner, I. (1997). *Psicología pastoral: Introducción a la praxis de la pastoral curativa.* Bilbao, Spain: Desclee de Brouwer.

Berry, J. W. (1980). "Acculturation as a Variety of Adaptation." In *Acculturation: Theory, Models and Some New Findings*, ed. A. M. Padilla, 9–25. Boulder, Colo.: Westview.

———. (1997). "Immigration, Acculturation and Adaptation." *Applied Psychology* 46:5–68.

Bertrando, P., and D. Toffanetti (2004). *Historia de la terapia familiar* [Family Therapy History]. Barcelona, España: Paidos.

Beutler, L. E., M. Malik, S. Alimohamed, T. M. Harwood, H. Talebi, S. Noble, et al. (2004). "Therapist Variables." In *Handbook of Psychotherapy and Behavior Change*, ed. M. Lambert, 227–306. New York: Wiley.

Bigge, M. L., and S. S. Shermis (2004). *Learning Theories for Teachers.* Boston: Pearson.

Bloom, B. L. (1981). "Focused Single-Session Therapy: Initial Development and Evaluation." In *Forms of Brief Therapy*, ed. S. Budman, 167–216. New York: Guilford.

Blum, L. (2002). *"I'm Not a Racist, But . . .": The Moral Quandary of Race.* Ithaca, N.Y.: Cornell University Press.

Boff, L. (2001). *Ética planetaria desde el Gran Sur.* Madrid: Editorial Trotta.

———. (2002). *El águila y la gallina: Una metáfora de la condición humana.* Madrid: Editorial Trotta.

Boisen, A. T. (1936). *Exploration of the Inner World.* New York: Harper and Brothers.

Brea, J. A. (2003, March). "Population Dynamics in Latin America." *Population Bulletin* 58 (1). Washington, D.C.: Population Reference Bureau.

Bridgers, B., P. M. Brown, J. Breger, and H. A. Roark (1997). "Cross-Cultural Consideration in Family Preservation Practice." In *Cross-Cultural Practice with Couples and Families*, ed. P. M. Brown and J. S. Shalett, 141–58. New York: Haworth.

Briones, D. F., P. L. Heller, H. P. Chalfant, A. E. Roberts, S. F. Aguirre-Hauchbaum, and W. F. Farr (1990). "Socioeconomic Status, Ethnicity, Psychological Distress and Readiness to Utilize a Mental Health Facility." *American Journal of Psychiatry* 147:1333–40.

Bronfenbrenner U. (1979). *The Ecology of Human Development.* Cambridge, Mass.: Harvard University Press.

Buber, M. (1999). *Martin Buber on Psychology and Psychotherapy: Essays, Letters, and Dialogue.* Syracuse, N.Y.: Syracuse University Press.

Carlson, D. L. (1994). *Why Do Christians Shoot Their Wounded? Helping (Not Hurting) Those with Emotional Difficulties.* Downers Grove, Ill.: InterVarsity.

Casas, J. M., and S. D. Pytluck (1995). "Hispanic Identity Development: Implications for Research and Practice." In *Handbook of Multicultural Counseling*, ed. J. G. Ponterotto, J. M. Casas, L. A. Suzuki, and C. M. Alexander, 155–80. Thousand Oaks, Calif.: Sage.

Casas, J. M., M. J. Vasquez, and C. A. Ruiz de Esparza (2002). "Counseling the Latina/o: A Guiding Framework for a Diverse Population." In *Counseling across Cultures*, ed. P. B. Pederson, J.

G. Draguns, W. J. Looner, and J. E. Trimble, 133–59. Thousand Oaks, Calif.: Sage.

Cassell, E. (1992). "The Nature of Suffering: Physical, Psychological, Social, and Spiritual Aspects." In *The Hidden Dimension of Illness: Human Suffering*, ed. P. L. Stark and J. P. McGovern. New York: National League for Nursing Press.

Cauce, A. M., and M. Domenech-Rodriguez (2002). "Latino Families: Myths and Realities." In *Latino Children and Families in the United States: Current Research and Future Directions*, ed. J. M. Contreras, K. A. Kerns, and A. M. Neal-Barnett, 3–25. Westport, Conn.: Praeger.

Comas-Diaz, L. (2001). "Hispanics, Latinos or *Americanos*: The Evolution of Identity." *Cultural Diversity and Ethnic Minority Psychology* 7 (2): 115–20.

Combs, A. W. (1986). "What Makes a Good Helper? A Person Centred Approach." *Person Centred Review* 1 (1): 51–61.

Cormier, L. S. and H. Hackney. (2005). *Counseling Strategies and Interventions*. Boston: Allyn and Bacon.

Cox, O. C. (2000). *Race: A Study in Social Dynamics*. New York: Monthly Review.

Crooks, R., and K. Baur (2005). *Our Sexuality*. Philadelphia: Wadsworth.

Davis, H. (2005). "Cultural Transmission of Social Knowledge in Preschool: A Costa Rican Perspective." In *Learning in Cultural Context: Family, Peers, and School*, ed. A. E. Maynard and M. I. Martini, 133–51. New York: Kluwer Academic / Plenum.

De la Torre, M. A. (2003). *Reading the Bible from the Margins*. Maryknoll, N.Y.: Orbis.

Del Carril, B. (1991). *El bautismo de América*. Buenos Aires: Emece Editores.

Delgado, R., and J. Stefancic (1998). *The Latino/a Condition: A Critical Reader*. New York: New York University Press.

Diagnostic and Statistical Manual of Mental Disorders (DSM-IV-TR) (2000). Washington, D.C.: American Psychiatric Association.

Eckes, T., H. Trautner, and R. Behrendt (2005). "Gender, Subgroups, and Intergroup Perception: Adolescents' Views of Own-Gender and Other-Gender Groups." *Journal of Social Psychology* 145 (1): 85–111 (accessed June 28, 2005, from EBSCO database).

Egan, G. (2002). *The Skilled Helper*. Pacific Grove, Calif.: Brooks/ Cole.

Ekman, P., and W. V. Friesen (1975). *Unmasking the Face: A Guide to Recognizing Emotions from Facial Clues*. Englewood Cliffs, N.J.: Prentice Hall.

Falicov, C. J. (1996). "Mexican Families." In *Ethnicity and Family Therapy*, ed. M. McGoldrick, J. Giordano, and J. Pearce, 169– 82. New York: Guilford.

———. (1998). *Latino Families in Therapy: A Guide to Multicultural Practice*. New York: Guilford.

Fasching, D. J., and D. Dechant (2001). *Comparative Religious Ethics: A Narrative Approach*. Malden, Mass.: Blackwell.

Feagin, J. R., and C. B. Feagin (1999). *Racial and Ethnic Relations*. Upper Saddle River, N.J.: Prentice Hall.

Fernández-Armesto, F. (2003). *The Americas: A Hemispheric History*. New York: Ballantine.

Findley, M. J., and H. M. Cooper (1983). "Locus of Control and Academic Achievement: A Literature Review." *Journal of Personality and Social Psychology* 44:419–27.

Flores, E., J. M. Tschann, B. VanOss Marin, and P. Pantoja (2004, February). "Marital Conflict and Acculturation among Mexican American Husbands and Wives." *Cultural Diversity and Ethnic Minority Psychology* 10 (1): 39–52.

Flores, M. T. (2000). "La familia Latina." In *Family Therapy with Hispanics: Toward Appreciating Diversity*, ed. M. T. Flores and G. Carey, 3–28. Boston: Allyn and Bacon.

Freire, P. (1992). *Pedagogy of Hope: Reliving Pedagogy of the Oppressed*. Trans. R. R. Barr. New York: Continuum.

———. (2000). *Pedagogy of the Oppressed*. Trans. M. Bergman Ramos. New York: Continuum. Original work published 1970.

Garcia, I. (1997). Dignidad: *Ethics through Hispanic Eyes*. Nashville, Tenn.: Abingdon.

Gladding, S. T. (2002). *Family Therapy: History, Theory and Practice*, 3rd ed. Upper Saddle River, N.J.: Prentice Hall.

Gloria, A. M., and J. J. Peregoy (1996). "Counseling Latino Alcohol and Other Drug Abusers: Cultural Issues for Consideration." *Journal of Substance Abuse Treatment* 13:1–8.

Goldenberg, H., and I. Goldenberg (2002). *Counseling Today's Families*. Pacific Grove, Calif.: Brooks/Cole.

González, J. L. (1990). Mañana: *Christian Theology from a Hispanic Perspective*. Nashville, Tenn.: Abingdon.

———. (1992). *Out of Every Tribe and Nation: Christian Theology at the Ethnic Roundtable*. Nashville, Tenn.: Abingdon.

———. (2003). *Historia del cristianismo 2*. Miami: Editorial Unilit.

Gracia, J. J. E., and P. De Greiff (2000). *Hispanics/Latinos in the United States: Ethnicity, Race, and Rights*. New York: Routledge.

Greenberg, J. S., C. E. Bruess, and D. W. Haffner (2002). *Exploring the Dimensions of Human Sexuality*. Sudbury, Mass.: Jones and Bartlett.

Greenberg, L. S. (2004). "Emotion-Focused Therapy." *Clinical Psychology and Psychotherapy* 11 (1): 3–14.

Gutiérrez, G. (1985). *On Job: God-Talk and the Suffering of the Innocent*. Maryknoll, N.Y.: Orbis.

———. (1994). *A Theology of Liberation: History, Politics, and Salvation*. Ed. and trans. C. Inda and J. Eagleson. New York: Orbis.

Hanna, S. M., and J. H. Brown (1999). *The Practice of Family Therapy: Key Elements across Models*, Belmont, Calif.: Wadsworth.

Herman, K. C. (1993). "Reassessing Predictors of Therapist Competence." *Journal of Counseling and Development* 72 (1): 29–32.

Hershenson, D. B., P. W. Power, and M. Waldo (1996). *Community Counseling: Contemporary Theory and Practice*. Boston: Allyn and Bacon.

Heschel, A. J. (1976). *God in Search of Man: A Philosophy of Judaism*. New York: Farrar, Straus and Giroux.

Hesse, H. (1943/1982). *Magister Ludi*. New York: Bantam.

Hick, J. H. (1990). *Philosophy of Religion*. Englewood Cliffs, N.J.: Prentice Hall.

Holt, T. (2000). *The Problem of Race in the 21st Century*. Cambridge, Mass.: Harvard University Press.

Horowitz, R. (1997). "The Expanded Family and Family Honor." In *The Family Experience: A Reader in Cultural Diversity*, ed. M. Hutter. Boston: Allyn and Bacon.

Howe, L. T. (1995). *The Image of God: A Theology for Pastoral Care and Counseling*. Nashville, Tenn.: Abingdon.

Hurtado, A. (1995). "Variations, Combinations, and Evolutions: Latino Families in the United States." In *Understanding Latino Families: Scholarship, Policy, and Practice*, ed. R. E. Zambrana, 41–61. Thousand Oaks, Calif.: Sage.

James, W. (1902/2004). *The Varieties of Religious Experience*. Repr. New York: Barnes and Noble.

Jones, J. M. (1997). *Prejudice and Racism*. New York: McGraw-Hill.

Jordan, J. V. (2000). "A Model of Connection for a Disconnected World." In *Odysseys in Psychotherapy*, ed. J. Shay and J. Wheelis. New York: Ardent Media.

Kaplan, H. (1974). *Disorders of Sexual Desire*. New York: Brunner/Mazel.

Kilty, K. M., and M. V. De Haymes (2000). "Racism, Nativism, and Exclusion: Public Policy, Immigration, and the Latino Experience in the United States." In *Latino Poverty in the New Century: Inequalities, Challenges, and Barriers*, ed. M. V. De Haymes, K. M. Kilty, and E. A. Segal, 1–25. New York: Haworth.

King, M. L. Jr. (1963, April 16). *Letter from Birmingham Jail*. In "Nobel Peace Prize Winners, 2005 to 1901," *The Nobel Prize Internet Archive*, http://www.nobelprizes.com/nobel/peace/MLK-jail .html (accessed on September 11, 2005). Dr. King wrote this letter as a response to a published statement by eight fellow clergymen from Alabama (Bishop C. C. J. Carpenter, Bishop Joseph A. Durick, Rabbi Hilton L. Grafman, Bishop Paul Hardin, Bishop Holan B. Harmon, the Reverend George M. Murray, the Reverend Edward V. Ramage, and the Reverend Earl Stallings).

Kinsey, A., W. Pomeroy, and C. Martin (1948). *Sexual Behavior in the Human Male*. Philadelphia: Saunders.

Kivinen, O., and P. Ristela (2003). "From Constructivism to a Pragmatist Conception of Learning." *Oxford Review of Education* 29 (3): 363–75.

Kleinman, A. (1988). *The Illness Narratives: Suffering, Healing, and the Human Condition*. New York: Basic.

Knowles, M., E. Holton, and R. Swanson (2005). *The Adult Learner: The Definitive Classic in Adult Education and Human Resource Development*. 6th ed. San Diego, Calif.: Elsevier.

Kohlhasen, C. W. (1995). "The Influence of Cultural and Religious Orientations on Latino Attitudes toward Illness, Suffering, and Death: Implications for Medical Decision-Making." University of Michigan, Ann Arbor, Mich.: UMI Dissertation Services, nr. 9625021 (photocopy, 1997).

LaFromboise, T., H.L.K. Coleman, and J. Gerton, (1993). "Psychological Impact of Biculturalism: Evidence and Theory." *Psychological Bulletin*, 114 (3): 395–412.

Lambert, M. J. (1986). "Implications of Psychotherapy Outcome Research for Eclectic Psychotherapy." In *Handbook of Eclectic Psychotherapy*, ed. J. C. Norcros. New York: Brunner-Routledge, 436–62.

Langberg, D. M. (1997). *Counseling Survivors of Sexual Abuse*. Wheaton, Ill.: Wheaton House.

Larson, D. B., and S. S. Larson (1994). *The Forgotten Factor in Physical and Mental Health: What Does the Research Show?* Rockville, Md.: National Institute of Healthcare Research.

Lawrence, R. J. (1989). *The Poisoning of Eros: Sexual Values in Conflict*. New York: Augustine Moore.

Lazarus, A. (2000). "My Professional Journey: The Development of Multimodal Therapy." In *Odysseys in Psychotherapy*, ed. J. Shay and J. Wheelis. New York: Ardent.

Lee, W. M. L. (1999). *An Introduction to Multicultural Counseling*. Philadelphia: Taylor and Francis.

Lefcourt, H. M. (1982). *Locus of Control: Current Trends in Theory and Research*. Hillsdale, N.J.: Erlbaum.

Levin, R. J. (2002). "The Physiology of Sexual Arousal in the Human Female: A Recreational and Procreational Synthesis." *Archives of Sexual Behavior* 31:405–11.

Lewis, J. A., and M. D. Lewis (1983). *Community Counseling: A Human Services Approach*. New York: Wiley.

Leyendecker, B., and M. E. Lamb (1999). "Latino Families." In *Parenting and Child Development in "Nontraditional" Families*, ed. M. E. Lamb, 247–62. Hillsdale, N.J.: Erlbaum.

Lockhart, J., and S. B. Schwartz (1984). *Early Latin America: A History of Colonial Spanish America and Brazil*. New York: Cambridge University Press.

Luborsky, L., L. Diguer, D. A. Seligman, R. Rosenthal, E. D. Krause, S. Johnson, et al. (1999). "The Researcher's Own Therapy Allegiances: A 'Wild Card' in Comparisons of Treatment Efficacy." *Clinical Psychology: Science and Practice* 6:96–106.

Luepnitz, D. A. (1988). *The Family Interpreted: Feminist Theory in Clinical Practice*. New York: Basic.

Marcel, G. (1950). *The Mystery of Being*. London: Dacre.

Marger, M. N. (1994). *Race and Ethnic Relations: American and Global Perspectives*. Belmont, Calif.: Wadsworth.

Marin, G., and B. V. Marin (1991). *Research with Hispanic Populations*. Newbury Park, Calif.: Sage.

Marin, H. (2003). "Hispanics and Psychiatric Medications: An Overview." *Psychiatric Times* 20 (10): 80–83.

Masters, W. H., and V. E. Johnson (1961). "Orgasm, Anatomy of the Female." In *Encyclopedia of Sexual Behavior* 2, ed. A. Ellis and A. Abarbonel, 792-805. New York: Hawthorn.

————. (1966). *Human Sexual Response.* Boston: Little and Brown.

————. (1970). *Human Sexual Inadequacy.* Boston: Little and Brown.

————. (1976). *The Pleasure Bond.* New York: Bantam.

Matsumoto, D. (1994). *People: Psychology from a Cultural Perspective.* Pacific Grove, Calif.: Brooks/Cole.

Mayer, R. (1987). *Educational Psychology: A Cognitive Approach.* Boston: Little, Brown.

Michelson, M. R. (2003). "The Corrosive Effect of Acculturation: How Mexican Americans Lose Political Trust." *Social Science Quarterly* 84 (4): 918–33.

Miller, P. C., H. M. Leftcourt, J. G. Holmes, E. E. Ware, and W. E. Saley (1986). "Marital Locus of Control and Marital Problem Solving." *Journal of Personality and Social Psychology* 31:430–41.

Miller, R. B. (2004). *Facing Human Suffering: Psychology and Psychotherapy as Moral Engagement.* Washington, D.C.: American Psychological Association.

Minuchin, S. (1974). *Families and Family Therapy.* Cambridge, Mass.: Harvard University Press.

Minuchin, S., and H. C. Fishman (1984/2004). *Tecnicas de terapia familiar* [Family Therapy Techniques]. Repr. Barcelona: Paidos.

Miracle, T. S., A. W. Miracle, and R. F. Baumeister (2003). *Human Sexuality: Meeting Your Basic Needs.* Upper Saddle River, N.J.: Prentice Hall.

Mirandé, A. (1997). Hombres y machos: *Masculinity and Latino Culture.* Boulder, Colo.: Westview.

Moltmann, J. (2000). *Experiences in Theology: Ways and Forms of Christian Theology.* Trans. M. Kohl. Minneapolis: Fortress Press.

Montalvo, F. (1991). *Phenotyping, Acculturation, and Biracial Assimilation of Mexican Americans: Empowering Hispanic Families; A Critical Issue for the '90s.* Milwaukee, Wis.: Family Services America.

Montilla, R. E. (2004). *Viviendo la tercera edad: Un modelo integral de consejería para el buen envejecimiento*. Barcelona: Editorial Clie.

———. (2005). "Grieving and Reconnecting in Community." In *Reflections on Grief and Spiritual Growth*, ed. A. J. Weaver and H. Stone. Nashville, Tenn.: Abingdon.

Moore, T. (1992). *Care of the Soul: A Guide for Cultivating Depth and Sacredness in Everyday Life*. New York: HarperCollins.

Morin, E. (1999). *Seven Complex Lessons in Education for the Future*. Paris: UNESCO.

Morreale, S. P., B. H. Spitzberg, and J. K. Barge (2001). *Human Communication: Motivation, Knowledge, and Skills*. Belmont, Calif.: Wadsworth.

Moyerman, D. R., and B. D. Forman (1992). "Acculturation and Adjustment: A Meta-Analytic Study." *Hispanic Journal of Behavioral Sciences* 14:163–200.

Nelson, G., J. Lord, and J. Ochocka (2001). *Shifting the Paradigm in Community Mental Health: Towards Empowerment and Community*. Toronto: Toronto University Press.

Okun, B. F., J. Fried, and M. Okun (1999). *Understanding Diversity: A Learning-as-Practice Primer*. Pacific Grove, Calif.: Brooks/Cole.

Olson, R. E. (2002). *The Mosaic of Christian Beliefs: Twenty Centuries of Unity and Diversity*. Downers Grove, Ill.: InterVarsity.

Ormond, J. E. (1995). *Educational Psychology: Principles and Applications*. Englewood Cliffs, N.J.: Prentice Hall.

Paniagua, F. A. (2004). "Culturally Sensitive Mental Health Services for Latino or Hispanic Families." *PsycCritiques* (American Psychological Association).

Paolucci, H. (1962/1996). *The Political Writings of St. Augustine*. Repr. Washington, D.C.: Regnery.

Payne, R. K. (2001). *A Framework for Understanding Poverty*. Highlands, Tex.: Aha! Process.

Peterson, C., and L. C. Barrett. (1987). "Explanatory Style of Academic Performance among University Freshmen." *Journal of Personality and Social Psychology* 53:603–7.

Pew Hispanic Center. (2004). "Bilingualism." 2002 National Survey of Latinos. Washington, D.C.

Pietrofesa, J. J., A. Hoffman, H. H. Splete, and D. V. Pinto (1978). *Counseling: Theory, Research, and Practice*. Chicago: Rand McNally.

Prada, R. R. (1992). *Sexualidad y amor.* Santa Fe de Bogota, Colombia: Ediciones Paulinas.

Ramírez, R. R., and G. P. de la Cruz (2002). *The Hispanic Population in the United States, March 2002.* Washington, D.C.: U.S. Census Bureau.

Rappaport, J. (1990). "Research Methods and the Empowerment Social Agenda." In *Researching Community Psychology: Issues of Theory and Methods,* ed. P. Tolan, C. Keys, F. Chertok, and L. Jason, 51–63. Washington, D.C.: American Psychological Association.

Rashkow, I. N. (2000). *Taboo or Not Taboo: Sexuality and Family in the Hebrew Bible.* Minneapolis: Fortress Press.

Ridley, C. R., and S. Udipi (2002). "Putting Cultural Empathy into Practice." In *Counseling across Cultures,* ed. P. B. Pederson, J. G. Draguns, W. J. Looner, and J. E. Trimble, 317–36. Thousand Oaks, Calif.: Sage.

Rivers, R. Y., and C. A. Morrow (1995). "Understanding and Treating Ethnic Minority Youth." In *Psychological Interventions and Cultural Diversity,* ed. J. F. Aponte, R. Y. Rivers, and J. Wohl, 164–80. Boston: Allyn and Bacon.

Roberts, A. (2000). "An Overview of Crisis Theory and Crisis Intervention." In *Crisis Intervention Handbook: Assessment, Treatment, and Research,* ed. A. Roberts, 3–30. New York: Oxford University Press.

Rogers, C. R. (1957). "The Necessary and Sufficient Conditions of Therapeutic Personality Change." *Journal of Consulting Psychology* 21:95–103.

Rogoff, B. (2003). *The Cultural Nature of Human Development.* New York: Oxford University Press.

Rojano, R. (2004). "The Practice of Community Family Therapy." *Family Process* 43 (1): 59–77.

Rothenberg, P. S. (1988). *Racism and Sexism: An Integrated Study.* New York: St. Martin's.

———. (2001). *Race, Class, and Gender in the United States: An Integrated Study.* New York: Worth.

Santiago-Rivera, A. L., P. Arredondo, and M. Gallardo-Cooper (2002). *Counseling Latinos and la Familia: A Practical Guide.* Thousand Oaks, Calif.: Sage.

Santrock, J. W. (2004). *Educational Psychology.* Boston: McGraw-Hill.

Schaefer, R. T. (2000). *Racial and Ethnic Groups*. 8th ed. Upper Saddle River, N.J.: Prentice Hall.

Schunk, D. (2004). *Learning Theories: An Educational Perspective*. 4th ed. Upper Saddle River, N.J.: Prentice Hall.

Sigelman, C. K., and E. A. Rider (2003). *Life-Span Human Development*. Belmont, Calif.: Wadsworth.

Skinner, B. F. (1968). *The Technology of Teaching*. Englewood Cliffs, N.J.: Prentice Hall.

Smith, R. L., and R. E. Montilla (2005). *Counseling and Family Therapy with Latino Populations: Strategies That Work*. Independence, Ky.: Routledge.

Smith, R. L., and P. Stevens-Smith (1992). *Family Counseling and Therapy: Major Issues and Topics*. Ann Arbor, Mich.: ERIC Counseling and Personnel Services Clearinghouse.

Smith, T. B., P. S. Richards, H. MacGranley, and F. Obiakor (2004). "Practicing Multiculturalism." In *Practicing Multiculturalism: Affirming Diversity in Counseling and Psychology*, ed. T. B. Smith, 3–16. Boston: Pearson.

Soelle, D. (1975). *Suffering*. Trans. E. R. Kalin. Philadelphia: Fortress Press.

Sofield, L., R. Hammett, and C. Juliano (1998). *Building Community: Christian, Caring, Vital*. Notre Dame, Ind.: Ave Maria.

Sternberg, R. (1996). "A Triangular Theory of Love." Psychological Review, 93, 119–125.

Suarez-Orozco, M. M., and M. M. Páez (2002). *Latinos: Remaking America*. Los Angeles: University of California Press.

Sue, D. W., and D. Sue (2003). *Counseling the Culturally Diverse: Theory and Practice*, 4th ed. New York: Wiley.

Tangney, J. P., R. F. Baumeister, and A. L. Boone (2004). "High Self-Control Predicts Good Adjustment, Less Pathology, Better Grades, and Interpersonal Success." *Journal of Personality* 72:271–324.

Tannenbaum, D. G., and D. Schultz (1998). *Inventors of Ideas: An Introduction to Western Political Philosophy*. New York: St. Martin's.

Therrien, M. and R. R. Ramírez. (2001). "The Hispanic Population in the United States: Population Characteristics, March 2000." *Current Population Survey*, P20-535. Washington, D.C.: U.S. Census Bureau.

Thomas, A., and S. Sillen (1972). *Racism and Psychiatry*. New York: Carol.

Torres, C. P. (2001). *Equidad en salud: Una mirada desde la perspectiva de la etnicidad*. Washington, D.C.: Programa de Políticas Públicas y Salud, División de Salud y Desarrollo Humano OPS/OMS. Public Health and Policy Program, Department of Health and Human Services.

Tournier, P. (1964/1999). *The Meaning of Persons*. Cutchogue, N.Y.: Buccaneer.

Trible, P. (1978). *God and the Rhetoric of Sexuality*. Philadelphia: Fortress Press.

U.S. Census Bureau (2004, June 14). "Hispanic and Asian Americans Increasing Faster than Overall Population." Public Information Office.

U.S. Department of Education, National Center for Education Statistics (1998). *Stopouts or Stayouts? Undergraduates Who Leave College in Their First Year*, NCES 1999-087. Washington, D.C.: U.S. Government Printing Office.

———. (2001). *The Condition of Education*, NCES 2001-045, Washington, D.C.: U.S. Government Printing Office.

———. (2003). *Status and Trends in the Education of Hispanics*, NCES 2003-008. Washington, D.C.: U.S. Government Printing Office.

Van Wolde, E. (1997). *Stories of the Beginning: Genesis 1–11 and Other Creation Stories*. Ridgefield, Conn.: Morehouse.

Vega, W. A. (1990). "Hispanic Families in the 1980s: A Decade of Research." *Journal of Marriage and Family* 52 (4): 1015–24.

———. (1995). "The Study of Latino Families: A Point of Departure." In *Understanding Latino Families: Scholarship, Policy, and Practice*, ed. R. E. Zambrana, 3–17. Thousand Oaks, Calif.: Sage.

Vigotsky, L. S. (1926/1997). *Educational Psychology*. Trans. R. Silverman. Repr. Boca Raton, Fla.: St. Lucie.

Von Balthasar, H. (1988). *Dare We Hope "That All Men Be Saved"? With a Short Discourse on Hell*. San Francisco: Ignatius.

Wesley, A. K. (2002). "Sacralisation and Secularization: An Analysis of a Few Biblical Passages for Possible Racial Overtones and Ethnocentrism." *Asia Journal of Theology* 16 (2): 375–95.

Wiarda, H. J., and H. F. Kline (2001). *An Introduction to Latin American Politics and Development*. Boulder, Colo.: Westview.

Willie, C. V. and R. J. Reddick (2003). *A New Look at Black Families.* Blue Ridge Summit, Pa.: Altamira.

Witmer, J. M., and T. J. Sweeney (1992). "A Holistic Model for Wellness and Prevention over the Life Span." *Journal of Counseling and Development* 71:140–48.

Wuellner, W. H., and R. C. Leslie (1984). *The Surprising Gospel: Intriguing Psychological Insights from the New Testament.* Nashville, Tenn.: Abingdon.

Yalom, I. (2003). *The Gift of Therapy: An Open Letter to a New Generation of Therapists and Their Patients.* New York: Harper Perennial.

259.0896
M792

CPSIA information can be obtained at www.ICGtesting.com
Printed in the USA
LVOW060857061111

253720LV00003B/74/P